It's appropriate to round off this tour with a visit to the ecclesiastical counterpart of the Town Hall, the **Cathédrale Saint-Michel et Sainte-Gudule**. This imposing Gothic edifice was elevated to the status of cathedral in 1962. The choir dates back to 1226, the nave and transept were added later in the 14th and 15th centuries, and the chapels were built on subsequently. The fine French-style façade (quite a rare sight in Belgium) is dominated by two huge towers of Jan van Ruysbroeck, who also designed the magnificent tower of the Town Hall.

The church suffered destruction at the hands of Calvinists in the 16th century and later on by French revolutionaries, but it has preserved its noble silhouette, rising above the Treurenberg (Mountain of Tears) west of the Rue Royale.

Entering through the main door, the first impression you get is of the somewhat sombre choir, but you'll soon see that the transept and nave are suf-

fused with the gentle light of the lovely **stained-glass windows**. Above the choir, which is presently closed for restoration, are five marvellous 16th-century windows portraying the city's Spanish, Burgundian and Austrian rulers. The window in the southern transept features Louis II and his wife Marie of Habsburg, while that of the northern transept shows Charles V and his wife Isabella of Portugal. Both of these windows are currently undergoing restoration.

BRUSSELS

- A ✔ in the text denotes a highly recommended sight
- A complete A–Z of practical information starts on p.115
- Extensive mapping on cover flaps; Blueprint map on p.115

Printed in Switzerland by Weber SA, Bienne.

1st edition

Reprinted October 1997

**Although we make every effort to ensure the accuracy of the
information in this guide, changes do occur. If you have any new
information, suggestions or corrections to contribute, we would
like to hear from you. Please write to Berlitz Publishing at one
of the above addresses.**

Original text:	Jack Altman
Additional text:	Sissy Puttaerts, Hazel Clarke, Jacques Noterman
Editor:	Hazel Clarke, Lemisse Al-Hafidh
Photography:	Chris Coe, except pp.61, 90, 92, 94 Claude Huber, and pp. 12, 15, 19, 20, 96-97 © Berlitz
Cartography:	🌐 Falk-Verlag, Hamburg
Thanks to:	The Tourist and Information Office of Brussels (TIB) and the King's Press Attaché for their help in the preparation of this guide.
Cover photographs:	front: *detail of building, Grand-Place* © The Image Bank back: *Grand-Place façade* © The Image Bank
p.4 photograph:	*Strolling across the Isle* – Chris Coe

CONTENTS

The City and the People

The people of Brussels resolved long ago to have a good time, come what may, and their stoic enjoyment of life is very contagious. The city that laboured for centuries under a succession of foreign rulers has emerged as a capital of European business and politics, of the Atlantic alliance and, of course, of Belgium.

The mixture of roles and the invasion of hordes of business people, bureaucrats, Eurocrats, property developers, lawyers and brigadier-generals might have washed away the city's identity in a sea of paper, ink and computer cards, but Brussels has known quite a few invaders in its time – Roman legions, Spanish Inquisitors, the armies of the Habsburgs, Napoleon, the German Kaiser, and Hitler. Somehow the people's fierce independence, robust sense of humour and overriding scepticism prevail. Brussels simply smiles and shrugs; and you take it or leave it. If you agree to see Brussels as the natives do, as a town of lively old-fashioned working-class districts and smart bourgeois neighbourhoods tucked away behind new skyscrapers, a town of fine restaurants and lusty taverns, with some fascinating museums and beautiful parks, you will find a place of distinctive personality and real pleasure.

On a continent where most capitals' major landmarks are cathedrals or royal palaces, it's significant that Brussels' glories are secular and municipal – the magnificent Town Hall and the trade guildhalls which cluster round the Grand-Place. Brussels is a triumphal monument to bourgeois prosperity snatched repeatedly from the ravages of bombardment, revolution and occupation.

The people's long-standing Catholic tradition is comfortably coupled with an exuberantly profane attitude to life. There's nothing delicate or introverted about a constitution which thrives on a diet of beer, mussels and *frites*. That's the **5**

workaday menu; life à la carte exhibits a culinary finesse and innovation that concedes nothing to the French. In addition, the town's prosperity is manifest in the elegance of the chic boutiques along the Avenue Louise and the Chaussée de Waterloo, as well as the bustle of the Place de Brouckère.

High days and feast days have always played an important role in the life of this city, handed down from the taste for bread and circuses introduced by the medieval dukes of Burgundy. The people of

Brussels love dressing up in costumes from all ages of their long history, from the guilds of the Middle Ages to the grand aristocracy of the Renaissance; everything is grist to their merry mill. There is something charming about a chubby, red-faced Fleming sporting the ruff, doublet and breeches of a Spanish hidalgo, or an embarrassed Walloon bank manager donning the rough linen shirt, leather apron and shiny boots of an ancestral leatherworker who distinguished himself in the guilds.

Many of the festivals are derived from religious holidays, but the most spectacular seem to be those, purely secular, which started with the citizens of the town proudly parading before a visiting ruler during a Joyeuse Entrée or Ommegang.

Yes, Brussels is bilingual, though with its huge foreign population, multilingual might be more accurate. While the rest of Belgium's 10 million inhabitants are divided between Dutch-speaking Flemings in the northern areas (57 percent of the population) and French-speaking Walloons in the south (33 percent), the capital (10 percent) seems to manage its own version of both. Meanwhile in the working-class neighbourhoods a *patois* has gradually evolved from Flemish mixed with French and a smattering of Spanish, and even a couple of words here and there of Hebrew. The street signs and public notices appear in both languages in the city (*Bruxelles/Brussel*), but the written language is generally French, spoken by 85% of its residents.

*C*afé theatre and pavement artists – part of the vibrant street culture of Brussels.

Those who like generalizations say the Walloons are talkative and perpetual malcontents (like the French?), the Flemings ponderous and mystical (like the Dutch?). But generalizations are generally false. Apart from a handful of extremists, there are few Flemings who would like to be **7**

Dutch, or Walloons who want to be French.

Though the national slogan is '*L'union fait la force*' (Unity is strength), it's a goal they're still working towards. Flemish-Walloon squabbles do continue, but some reconciliation is to be found in Brussels' official bilingualism and international status. The European Parliament, the various institutions of the European Union, NATO and its associated organizations, and private international companies have brought around 230,000 foreigners to Brussels, including over 100 nationalities, where they make up nearly one in four of the total population.

Brussels is a light, airy capital of over one million people. Only the town centre is actually named 'Brussels', the rest of the city is made up of 18 autonomous boroughs with their own mayors and police forces. Each has a distinctive identity and tradition – liberal, conservative or socialist; working-class or bourgeois. Since the 19th century, urban planning has thrust many wide avenues from the dense city centre to the spacious boulevards circling the periphery. The parks are innumerable and splendid.

The huge Palais de Justice, a symbol of Belgium's 19th-century self-assertion, finds its counterpart in the skyscrapers of today's multinational empires. The museums proudly display the glories of old Flemish masters, but the strong and solid subjects of those paintings, peasant and burgher alike, can still be seen wandering the backstreets just off the Grand-Place.

Yet apart from the festive set-pieces of historical pageantry, the city is very much one of the 20th century, accepting the present in a matter-of-fact way with few nostalgic glances to the past. The true symbol of modern Brussels is the Atomium, the huge model of an iron molecule represented by nine aluminium-covered spheres, which is a remnant of the 1958 World's Fair. Its slogan was '*Bilan du monde pour un monde plus humain*' (Balance of the world for a more humane world).

Brussels is the town of the good-natured comic-strip adventurer Tintin, and was also home to the bittersweet balladeer Jacques Brel. But it's known above all as the town of Pieter Brueghel. *The Fall of Icarus*, his masterpiece, in the Musées Royaux des Beaux-Arts is a delightful illustration of Brussels' affirmative spirit: a man goes on ploughing and a shepherd dreamily tends his flock while poor old Icarus, who flew too near the sun and melted his waxen wings, falls unnoticed into the sea. Life goes on.

*B*russels is a true haven for green, open spaces in which you can take a stroll, or just relax after a hard day sight-seeing.

A Brief History

In 57 BC Julius Caesar came to Belgium, saw it and, after a lot of trouble with what he said were 'the bravest of all the peoples of Gaul', conquered it. At that time, Brussels did not yet exist as a city, although two Roman roads had been built through its present site, one of which is still called Chaussée Romaine. From the evidence of the bronzes, coins and funeral urns found along the Chaussée de Haecht and the Rue Haute, a few dignitaries and officers built villas in the area some decades later.

During the 450 years of Roman rule, the Belgae of the southern region became heavily Latinized, while the north was left to Germanic tribes.

Brussels was first heard of in AD 695, when the bishop of Cambrai fell ill there during a tour of his diocese. Brosella it was called then, but was later known variously as Brucella, Bruocsella, Bruohsella, Bruesella and Borsella, with as **10** many different meanings sug-gested by historians – from 'stork's nest' to 'dwelling near the bridge'– though the most generally accepted seems to be 'dwelling in the marshes'. This supposedly refers to the three swampy islands in the (now paved-over) River Senne on which the first castle and church were built.

The Middle Ages

The foundation of the city proper dates back officially to AD 979 when Charles de Lotharingie, the brother of King Lothaire of France, erected a fortress there.

In the following century the town began to look more like a town when, in 1047, Count Lambert II of Louvain built a new castle on the Coudenberg heights (today called the Place Royale), surrounded by a group of houses within a walled-in compound. These dwellings were reserved for the count's knights and administrators; lack of space meant that less fortunate artisans and peasants were left unprotected outside the ramparts, thus lay-

HISTORICAL LANDMARKS

AD 979 Founding of the city with the construction of a fortress.

1047 Construction of the first city wall.

1303 Uprising of craftsmen demanding greater say in city government. (They were defeated in 1306.)

1401 Construction of the Town Hall begins.

1406 Dukes of Burgundy take control of Brussels.

1515 The Archduke of Brabant, the future Charles V, is emancipated.

1555 Charles V abdicates. Brussels subject to Philip II of Spain.

1568 Philip's governor of the Low Countries beheads Belgian counts Egmont and Hoorn for high treason.

1577 Brussels, with the Prince of Orange, revolts and drives out the Spanish, but they re-occupy the city in 1585.

1599 Archduchess Isabella (daughter of Philip II) and her husband reside and restore order in Brussels.

1695 Louis XIV of France bombards Brussels.

1715 Under the Treaty of Utrecht, Brussels becomes subject to Austria.

1789 Brabantine Revolution in Brussels drives the Austrians out, but is crushed the next year by Austria and France.

1795 Belgium is annexed by France.

1815 French defeated at Waterloo. Congress of Vienna puts Belgium under Dutch rule; William of Orange crowned.

1830 The Belgian Revolution begins in Brussels, leading to independence.

1831 Leopold of Saxe-Coburg made first King of the Belgians.

1835 First continental railway line is built between Brussels and Mechelen.

1914 Brussels occupied by Kaiser Wilhelm's German army.

1951 King Leopold III abdicates in favour of his son, Baudouin.

1957 EEC (now EU) makes its headquarters in Brussels.

1967 NATO headquarters moves to Brussels.

1993 King Baudouin succeeded by King Albert II.

ing the foundations for the long struggle between the city's haves and have-nots.

In the 12th century Brussels rose to prominence in the province of Brabant, gaining in prosperity due to its role as a way-station on the busy commercial route between the thriving trade centres of Cologne and Bruges. Visiting traders greatly esteemed the town for the skills of its goldsmiths and silversmiths.

By 1235 the city's administration was in the hands of an oligarchy of seven patrician families known as *lignages*. Each contributed an *échevin* or alderman to serve under the prince. Brussels expanded its trade in precious metals with international orders for minting coins. It also started a prosperous textile industry using wool imported from England.

Ommegang pageant was originally a religious celebration centred on a miraculous statue.

A number of *béguinages* (nunneries) were set up outside the city and were used by the textile manufacturers as a source of docile and cheap labour at a time when male workers were causing trouble with demands for higher wages and better working conditions.

The Brussels bourgeoisie was already growing prosperous and wilful. In 1291 Duke Jean I had to make tax and toll concessions to their municipal treasury. In an attempt to forestall the problems of dealing with recalcitrant artisans, the aldermanic oligarchy claimed the right of approval or veto over the formation of the craft guilds – a restriction that riled the artisans. The Brussels craftsmen, led by the weavers and fullers, staged a revolt demanding a greater say in city government. (They were to be inspiration some years later to their brothers in Bruges who victoriously rose against their French masters at the Battle of the Golden Spurs (*Eperons d'Or*) in 1302.) Some 36 professional groups were each allowed to send a 'master of the commune' and 'jurors' to participate in administering the town's affairs. Brussels' first attempt at democracy came to an abrupt end just three years later when the army of Duke Jean II and the patrician cavalry of the *lignages* defeated the artisans in the bloody battle of Vilvorde (1306).

For the next 50 years the artisans were forbidden to bear arms, and weavers and fullers were not allowed within the city limits after nightfall. The pressures and uprisings rumbled on until guild privileges were gradually reinstated for certain professions.

The Burgundians

Under the dukes of Burgundy, who took control of Brussels at the end of the 14th century, good times were to be had, if not by one and all, at least by the patrician families and their cronies. When they went into battle, their picnic baskets (as listed in the municipal records) included vast quantities of eel, salmon pâté, trout, spices, and gallons of local **13** beer and Rhenish wine. In peace time, the *grande bourgeoisie* relaxed in the fashionable steam-baths (*étuves*) where they were tended by young girls who served them wine and massaged their aching bones until the first evening bell of the friary announced closing time. Women were allowed in taverns only on Fridays. If caught in there on any other day, they were fined a large sum of money and were obliged to relinquish their outer garment.

High-living and prudishness went hand in hand; the city's burghers resisted the establishment of a university in Brussels, because they feared for their daughters' precious virtue at the hands of the marauding intellectuals.

The demand for Brussels cloth declined as textiles manufactured in England became increasingly competitive, and it had practically disappeared from international markets by 1430. With no work many artisans were forced to leave town and the population dropped. However the city compensated for the collapse of the textile industry by turning to tapestry weaving. The best of the Brussels weavers were recruited and the demand for their skills became intense. Later, some of the French paid the Brussels craftsmen the highest of compliments by attempting to recreate their work for foreign markets, even counterfeiting the municipal trademark 'B.B.' (Bruxella in Brabantia) found at the corner of each authentic Brussels tapestry.

This Burgundian era was also a golden age for the arts – van Eyck, van der Weyden, Memling and Bouts being only the best known of a group of superb 15th-century Flemish painters. Civic pride was reflected in the great Gothic town halls which sprang up all over Belgium, though none ever surpassed Brussels' own great jewel on the Grand-Place

After the decline of the textile industry Brussels artisans turned to tapestry weaving.

(see p.26), surrounded by the equally grand guildhouses.

The dukes – Philip the Bold and Philip the Good – asserted their supremacy with pageants and great festivities to keep the people happy. However, their dominance began to disintegrate in wars with Louis XI of France, and before long the city was beset with troubles – revolts, famine and plague. Charles the Bold died at the Battle of Nancy in 1477, and was succeeded by his daughter Mary, who married Maximilian of Austria and thus brought the Habsburgs to Brussels.

Under the Habsburgs

In 1515, Maximilian's grandson, the future Charles V, made his *Joyeuse Entrée* into Brussels as its new archduke. He then moved into the palace at Coudenberg, which was to be his only fixed residence during his peripatetic reign as King of Spain and Holy Roman Emperor. Brussels became the capital of the Low Countries as well as a great European centre. It was here that in 1555 Charles V proclaimed his abdication from the throne in favour of his son Philip.

The great Dutch philosopher Erasmus also enjoyed the city's pleasant atmosphere, living for several months in an elegant house which still stands in Anderlecht. One of his guests was Albrecht Dürer. Also during the 16th century, Pieter Brueghel came to Brussels to paint his marvellous studies of life in the Low Countries. Brussels' thriving trade in luxury goods at this time was enhanced by the vogue of its lace-makers and the expertise of its highly-prized gunsmiths.

The Ommegang or 'walk-around', the most spectacular of Brussels' numerous festivities, gave the Renaissance nobility and gentry of Brussels a chance to show off their riches in a superb procession around the city. Originally a religious celebration of a miraculous statue of the Virgin brought to the city in 1348, it soon became an undisguised assertion of the nobility's civic authority. The high point in the long history of the Ommegang is generally considered to have been the event in 1549 when Charles V proudly introduced to the citizens of Brussels his son from Spain, who was to become their king, Philip II. The Ommegang is still held every year at the beginning of July, and takes place on the Grand-Place.

Inquisitions, Bombs and Beheadings

That moment of glorious pageant in fact heralded dark days to come for the capital of the Low Countries. It was during Charles' reign that the Calvinists arrived in Brussels, and the spiritual rebellion against Catholicism became identified with the nationalist rebellion against Spanish rule. Charles ordered heretics to be burned, lesser delinquents to be beheaded or drowned and their heads displayed on pikes as a lesson to other recalcitrants. Anyone denouncing a troublemaker would be rewarded with half this person's property.

Charles only dimly perceived the seriousness of this threat to Spanish power and was lax in enforcing his orders. Philip, who disliked the Belgians, was less easy-going. He brought in the Inquisitors and surrounded himself with Spanish soldiers, and blood began to flow.

Nationalist resistance was led by William of Nassau, Prince of Orange. Philip, who in 1559 had left Brussels for Madrid in disgust, sent the Duke of Alba – known as the 'bloody Duke' – to quash the revolt and Counts Egmont and Hoorn, more nationalists than rebels, were executed on the Grand-Place in 1568. However, the Prince of Orange was able to drive out the Spanish in 1576 and Brussels enacted ferocious anti-Catholic legislation. Religious holidays were banned, church processions forbidden, and priests became frightened to appear in public. In 1581 the Catholic religion itself was simply 'abolished'.

This outraged Philip, who sent a large army under the command of Alexander Farnese to re-occupy the city. **17**

With the Counter-Reformation came a flood of Jesuits, monks and nuns into Brussels to reinforce the Catholic presence. The southern provinces of the Low Countries finally returned to Spain and Catholicism, but the northern provinces (now the Netherlands) succeeded in breaking away and remained largely Protestant.

Under the rule of Philip's daughter, Archduchess Isabella, and her husband Archduke Albert of Austria, Brussels returned to a general semblance of order (1599-1633). Life in the capital became quite fashionable with a constant flow of ambassadors, generals, bishops and cardinals bringing a new cosmopolitan air to the court of the governors-general around the Sablon quarter.

In summer, the chic place to be on a Sunday was around the Coudenberg Palace (now the the Place Royale). The nobility also often took boat rides on the Willebroeck Canal, which had been constructed in 1561 to replace the unreliable River Senne as Brussels' link with the sea. The spirit of the age

found great artistic expression in the sumptuous and exalted contours of Flemish baroque, which reached its peak with the magnificent paintings of Peter Paul Rubens.

At this time, Brussels was a haven for political exiles – Marie de Medici, Christina of Sweden, the dukes of Bouillon and Vendôme and the sons of Charles I of England. However, by the end of the century it wasn't quite so safe. In 1695, Louis XIV of France took his revenge for the Dutch and English shelling of his coastal towns with the wanton bombardment of Brussels. Marshall de Villeroy's army of 70,000 men occupied Anderlecht and set up its cannons at the gate of Ninove. For two days, bombs and cannonballs fell on some 4,000 buildings, killing 1,000 people, but the city did not surrender. The Grand-Place was badly damaged, yet the Town Hall's superb bell-tower survived.

The Royal Mint was destroyed by the bombs and replaced by a new opera house, the Théâtre de la Monnaie, built by an enterprising Italian banker aptly named Giovanni-Paolo Bombarda. The city's civic pride quickly found the money and energy to rebuild the rest of the city but retained much of its old Renaissance and baroque style, thus giving the Grand-Place an architectural harmony that has made it one of the great urban glories of Europe.

For a taste of the past, take a trip in a horse-drawn coach around the historic city of Bruges.

Revolution to Revolution

Joseph II, the Habsburg Emperor, ruled Belgium in the last part of the 18th century with a form of enlightened despotism. His religious reforms and judicial liberalization upset the profoundly conservative Belgians, and the centralized Vienna-controlled administration jarred with their habit of local autonomy, and nowhere more than in Brussels.

This was at a time when the Americans had thrown off the British yoke and the French

19

were getting rid of their royal one. The old patrician families of Brussels staged a revolt which drove the Austrians out in January 1790 and restored ancient privileges under the 'Etats Belgiques Unis' (United Belgian States). Their reactionary regime was very short-lived; in December 1790, the Austrians returned, only to be ousted in 1792 by the French Revolutionary army under the leadership of General Dumouriez. In 1793, after the battle of Fleurus, the French decided simply to annex Belgium. They proclaimed the people of Brussels to be: '*frères et amis, tous citoyens, tous égaux en droits*' (brothers and friends, all citizens, all equal in rights) with devastating results. Museums and libraries were pillaged, factory equipment was requisitioned en masse, and all able-bodied men were press-ganged into the Revolutionary army.

Napoleon Bonaparte visited Brussels in July 1803. He was so determined to win over the populace, that he had the city's fountains flowing with wine,

flattered the leathercraftsmen by ordering their finest luggage, and bought a lace surplice for Pope Pius VII. Unlike Louis XIV's bombardment, Napoleon's visit did not have a dramatic physical effect on Brussels, but he did give the city the old ramparts, which had previously been the property of the state. One of the many benefits of 'Frenchification' as a result of his rule was also the whitewashing of the sombre brick façades to add more light to this northern outpost of his empire.

In the winter of 1813-14, Brussels saw the French troops depart, only for them to be replaced by a procession of Russians, Prussians, Dutch, and finally by the English, waiting for orders to go to battle with Napoleon in 1815. The rendezvous was around 12 miles away, at Waterloo, on 17 June. The day after the battle, Brussels was once again full of foreign troops, most of them half-dead.

Napoleon's defeat and the Congress of Vienna led to 16 years of Dutch rule for Belgium, resurrecting old tensions and creating new ones. During Napoleon's rule, the national language had been French. Even in Flanders, French was the language of the nobility and bourgeoisie and had been ever since the King of France was made its overlord. King William of Orange introduced Dutch, previously spoken only by the lower ranks of society, into all the schools, municipal governments and law courts. Six hundred bureaucrats and their families were forced to commute between the kingdom's two capitals, The Hague and Brussels, for parliamentary sessions. French-speaking teachers were upset by the imposition of Dutch and taught the sciences in Latin. Catholics were upset by the removal of schools from church control and the liberals were upset by press censorship. Brussels was ready for another revolution.

*N*ear the historic town of Waterloo, site of Napoleon's defeat on 17 June 1815.

21

Independence at Last

In February 1829, an opera by Daniel François Auber, entitled *La Muette de Portici*, had its *première* at the Théâtre de la Monnaie. The Dutch royal family attended the opening gala, but they didn't like what they saw: a rousing story of the Neapolitans' struggles against their oppressors, with an aria '*Amour sacré de la Patrie*' (Sacred love of the fatherland) wildly applauded by the Brussels audience. The opera was promptly withdrawn from the repertoire. Its resumption 18 months later was still too soon for Dutch tastes.

With Paris overthrowing its monarch in July 1830, revolution was in the air. The Brussels audience on 25 August, predominantly young intellectuals from the bourgeoisie, joined in the climactic aria and then left to team up with workers demonstrating against poverty and unemployment on the Place de la Monnaie. Rioters attacked the Palais de Justice, where liberal journalists were on trial for breaching the censorship laws, and sacked the homes of government ministers while police and army stood idly by.

The next day bakeries were raided for bread, the bars for alcohol, and machinery was smashed in the factories. The bourgeois rebellion for civil rights was threatening to turn into a fully fledged workers' revolt until Baron Vanderlinden d'Hooghvorst set up a militia of volunteers to protect properties from the riots – and, reinforced by supporters from Liège and other provincial cities, to fight the Dutch Army which King William had sent to Brussels in September. Many casualties on both sides ensued in what was known as the 'Belgian Revolution'.

Belgium gained her independence and on 21 July 1831 the keys of the capital were handed over to the country's new king, Leopold of Saxe-Coburg.

With independence came phenomenal economic growth together with social, political and religious conflicts. Tensions were high between

Catholics and liberals and between Flemings and Walloons. By resisting universal suffrage, conservative Catholic provinces maintained control over the government and fuelled their fight with the liberals of the capital over schools and church power.

Brussels was nominally bilingual, but in fact French was increasingly dominant in business, the sciences and state administration. The Flemings campaigned with increasing indignation for greater use of their language in the universities and the law courts.

Industrial expansion as well as imperial adventures in Africa, particularly in the Congo, brought great prosperity to Brussels, and there was a flurry of rebuilding, with magnificent mansions and brash commercial buildings rising up along the wide avenues and boulevards. As ever, the products of the luxury industries were at a premium: textiles, furniture, lace, fine porcelain, paper and books – the printing industry benefiting from the flourishing skulduggery of

*S*tatue of Fame on top of the Dome of the Maison des Boulangers (Au Roi d'Espagne).

Brussels publishers pirating new French best-sellers.

Brussels was once again a safe refuge for political exiles – Polish, Italian and French, and for Russia's Michael Bakunin and Germany's Friedrich Engels and Karl Marx (who were expelled from Paris in 1845). Marx and Engels organized the socialist German Workers' Club at Le Cygne on the Grand-Place, now a high-class restaurant with unsocialist prices. The two wrote the *Communist Manifesto* here – **23** and were kicked out of Belgium in 1848, when it was feared that their writings and ideas might reproduce the latest Paris revolution.

The emergence of Belgium as a nation in the 19th century also brought an explosion of artistic achievement in the capital. Painters including James Ensor, Félicien Rops and Fernand Khnopff came together in the Groupe des XX in 1883. Brussels was also a major centre of Art Nouveau architecture under the leadership of Victor Horta and Paul Hankar.

World Wars and International Leadership

Belgium's historic vulnerability to foreign invasion was displayed again in August 1914, when Brussels was occupied by Kaiser Wilhelm's German armies. The capital, led by the Mayor Adolphe Max, put up a heroic passive resistance to the German occupation. Max was deported to Germany after refusing to provide lists of the unemployed who would have been used as forced labour in German factories.

One of his wartime successors, Louis Steens, fought German attempts to enlist Flemish collaborators to 'deFrenchify' Brussels. When the Germans were defeated, Belgium expressed its new-found sense of national unity in the introduction of universal suffrage, the right to strike, a Flemish university and finally, a truce in the church-school conflict.

The 1930s saw the emergence in Brussels, as in other European capitals, of new fascist groups drawing on social discontent and primitive chauvinism – the Rex, Jeunesses Nationales, Légion Nationale and a Flemish group, the VNV, which appealed to the frustrations of Fleming workers in the capital. The fascist leader Léon Degrelle indeed achieved that which had eluded all other Belgian leaders – he united Catholics, liberals and socialists in a combined effort to defeat him, resoundingly, in the 1937 elections. These grim times offered the best breeding ground for a flight into the surrealist art of René Magritte and Paul Delvaux, and the inspired comic-strip escapism of Hergé's *Tintin*.

Then came World War II and another German occupation. The Nazi invaders found a few fascist collaborators to prepare Belgium for integration into the Reich – principally among the VNV, the Rexists and Heinrich Himmler's favourites, the Flemish fanatics of De Vlag. But while the 'Wallonie' and 'Langemark' divisions were sending Belgians off to die with the German army on the Eastern front, the Légion Nationale joined the underground movement *against* the Germans. Linked with the government-in-exile based in London, the Belgian resistance was active in organizing the escape of Jews and other residents whose lives were at risk, and in engineering an elaborate campaign of sabotage of the Nazi industrial war-machine by Groupe G, a band of engineering graduates from Brussels University.

After the war, Belgium held a referendum in which King Leopold III gained a majority of 58%; however, not having a majority in each province, he refused to be reinstated and was succeeded in 1951 by his son Baudouin. While Flemings and Walloons continued to squabble, Belgium took on a new role as the internationalist capital of western Europe and the Atlantic alliance. In 1957, the EEC (now the European Union) established its headquarters in Brussels. The following year, the city staged a very successful World's Fair based on the theme of building a better world for mankind.

NATO moved its headquarters to Brussels in 1967 and the city subsequently attracted around a quarter of a million permanent foreign residents to work in military organizations and the multinational offices of commerce. Brussels' own domestic ethnic balancing act is the perfect microcosm of the problems besetting the international institutions to which it is host, like a set of marriages in which the in-laws have to get on together for the sake of the children.

25

What to See

Brussels' centre starts at the famous Grand-Place, but on the way there you should visit its world-famous mascot, the **Manneken-Pis**. The little boy blithely peeing into a fountain on the Rue de l'Etuve is 61cm (24in) high, made of bronze, and was created in 1619 by Jérôme Duquesnoy. It will put you in the perfect mood to approach this city – with a sense of humour about the more solemn monuments in the city. This statue has come to symbolize Brussels' defiance of an often hostile world; he has been caricatured a number of times in the city's satirical magazines as hurrying defeated enemies on their way. Almost as impressive as the statue itself are the myriad versions of him to be found in surrounding souvenir shops – watering cans, bottle-stoppers and even odd little corkscrews.

Grand-Place

This is the true centre of town, the focus of the city's historic moments, and the most apt expression of its civic pride.

In the 10th century, when the heirs of Charlemagne were making Brussels their citadel, the Grand-Place, at the lower end of the then visible River Senne, was the town's *Nedermerct* (lower market). Today it still offers a colourful flower-market every day except Monday, and on Sunday mornings also a cheerful bird market. As

many of the surrounding street names still attest – the Rue Chair et Pain, du Poivre, des Harengs, and Marché aux Herbes, au Beurre and au Charbon – it was also once the busy commercial centre for meat, bread, pepper, herrings, spices, butter and charcoal.

In the old days tournaments were held here, with jousts and processions, both religious and secular. Today, the Ommegang (see p.103) is still celebrated on the Grand-Place at the beginning of July, as descendants of the great patrician families of Brussels don their costumes

Two of the most famous landmarks of Brussels; Mannekin-Pis (left) and the Grand-Place.

and parade around in the old style, with dances, acrobatics and a climax of human chess played out on a giant checkerboard painted on the paving stones. Even if you are not in town for the Ommegang, you can sit at one of the delightful outdoor cafés and imagine the pageant of bygone days. You may also remember that this **27** was the place where many important celebrities – such as the Count of Egmont in 1568 – were beheaded. (Nonentities were usually done away with on a mound at the site of the present Palais de Justice.)

These days the square is animated by music concerts and open-air theatre. The Grand-Place has not lost its festive tone – minus the executions – and remains the best people-watching spot in town. Some of the town's residents pretend they never go near the place, claiming that it's just for tourists, but in fact you'll find as many natives here as you will foreign visitors. Indeed the bright, red-cheeked faces in the many taverns are right out of Brueghel, and evidently local colour.

Apart from its lively atmosphere, the Grand-Place is quite simply an architectural masterpiece – for poet Jean Cocteau, 'the most beautiful square in the world'; for the rest of us, an undeniable visual joy and well worth a lengthy visit. Its harmony of Gothic, Renaissance and baroque styles was

achieved after the devastating bombardment by Louis XIV's artillery in 1695. The city fathers were forced to plan the restoration with a firm hand, ensuring the unity of its design. The guilds and corporations proudly cooperated in the dignified venture of reconstruction, sparing no expense on the pure gold-leaf façades which glow in the sun.

Louis' cannons, drawn up at the Porte de Ninove, took the soaring tower of the **Hôtel de Ville** (Town Hall) as their principal target, yet, miraculously, it was the one thing that actually survived. This tower, with its steeple rising 103m (295ft) above the ground, a piece of lace-like stonework both massive and graceful, was designed in the 15th century by Jan van Ruysbroeck. At the pinnacle is a fine statue-cum-vane in gilded copper (currently undergoing restoration) of the town's patron saint Michael heroically slaying the devil.

A major part of the Town Hall's charm derives from the off-centre placing of the tower and its entrance. On the right

BRUSSELS HIGHLIGHTS

Atomium: *bd. du Centenaire, 1020 Brussels.* Open (Sep-June) 10am-6pm; (July-Aug) 9.30am-6pm; BF200. Métro: Heysel. Tram: 23, 81. Bus: 84, 89. (See p.51)

Cathédrale Saint-Michel: *Parvis Sainte-Gudule, 1000 Brussels.* The choir is currently closed for restoration. Open summer 7am-7pm; winter 7am-6pm; BF30. tel: 219 6834. (See pp.37-39)

Church of Notre-Dame de la Chapelle: *4 rue des Ursulines, 1000 Brussels.* (See p.42)

Church of Notre-Dame du Sablon: *3B rue de la Régence, 1000 Brussels.* Open 9am-6pm. Tours on request. (See p.41)

Grand-Place: Central square surrounded by houses of the guilds and corporations and dominated by the Hôtel de Ville. (See p.26)

Hôtel de Ville (Town Hall): *Grand-Place, 1000 Brussels.* Open (Oct-March) Tue-Fri 9.30am-12.15pm and 1.45-4pm; (Apr-Sep) 1.45-5pm; Sunday and public holidays 10am-noon and 2-4pm. Guided tours only; BF75. Métro: Bourse, Gare Centrale. Tram: 52, 55, 81. Bus: 34, 48, 95, 96. (See p.28)

Palais de Justice (Law Courts): *pl. Poelaert, 1000 Brussels.* Open Mon-Fri 9am-4pm; Free. Guided tours on request. (See p.43)

Manneken Pis: *rue de l'Etuve, 1000 Brussels.* (See p.26)

Mini-Europe: *20 bd. du Centenaire, 1020 Brussels.* 300 models of well-known European sites. Open all year round 9.30am-6pm/8pm; BF380. Métro: Heysel. Tram: 23, 81. Bus: 84, 89. Belgian Railways trip 125 and Dutch Railways trip 3. (See p.106)

Musées Royaux des Beaux-Arts: Location of the Museums of Fine Arts and Modern Art (see p.45). Site of the Royal Library, *4 bd. de l'Empereur.* Métro: Gare Centrale, Parc. Tram: 92, 93, 94. Bus: 95, 96. (See p.44)

Palais du Roi (Royal Palace): *Place des Palais.* King's official office. Open (July-Sep) Tue-Sun 9.30am-3.30pm (check with tourist office as dates and times frequently change). (See p.44)

Royal Greenhouses: *Laeken.* Open (late April-early May) 9.30am-4pm (check with tourist office). Tram: 19, 23, 52, 92. Bus: 53. (See p.52)

Conseil Communal (Council Room) and its rich 18th-century tapestries (guided visits only). The Tourist and Information Office of Brussels (TIB), operates in the right wing of the building.

While the Gothic Town Hall may be the dominant feature, the square's elegant human scale is achieved by the magnificent houses of the guilds and corporations which emphasize the major role played in the city's past by its diligent and prosperous bourgeoisie. Start your tour on the west side at the corner of the Rue de la Tête d'Or.

The House of the Haberdashers, No. 7, known as **Le Renard** (The Fox), was rebuilt in 1699 in the classical style (initiated by Louis XIV, the man responsible for the building's destruction four years previously). A fine statue of St

wing, look out for three stone carvings on the capitals of the pillars: the 'Drinking Monks', the 'Sleeping Moor' accompanied by his harem and the 'Estrapade' (a torture in which the victim is dunked in liquid mud). The staircase found at the entrance of the left wing is flanked by splendid lions and the archway over the door features statues of eight biblical prophets. (The originals of these capitals and prophets are to be found in the municipal museum opposite.) Inside the Town Hall, visit the Salle du

Nicholas, patron of all haberdashers, tops it off. The House of the Boatmakers, at No. 6, bears their emblem, **Le Cornet** (The Horn), over the door. The gable below the roof is designed in the shape of a poop deck from a 17th-century galleon. Above the doorway of No. 5, the House of the Archers, **La Louve** (The She-wolf) is a bas-relief showing Romulus and Remus being suckled by the wolf-mother of Rome. This superb example of High Renaissance style contains four statues on the façade of the second storey representing Truth, Falsehood, Peace and Discord. No. 4, **Le Sac** (The Bag), House of the Coopers and Cabinet-makers, has one of the few façades which actually remained intact after

Finding Your Way

In the bilingual city of Brussels, street and building names appear in both French and Flemish, but for simplicity's sake we've used only the French (spoken by 80 percent of the population). For Flanders, where Flemish prevails, we've followed the local practice in citing place names. Here are some key terms with translations in the two languages to help you along.

English	French	Flemish
belfry	beffroi	belfort
bridge	pont	brug
castle	château	kasteel
church	église	kerk
convent	béguinage	begijnhof
hill	mont	heuvel
house	maison	huis
information	renseignements	inlichtingen
law courts	palais de justice	gerechtshof
square	place	plein, plaats
street	rue	straat

the severe bombardment. No. 3 is named **La Brouette** (The Wheelbarrow), House of the Grease-mechants. Nos. 1 and 2, **Au Roi d'Espagne** (The King of Spain), a classical Italian-style House of the Bakers, bears a statue of Fame on top of its octagonal dome.

On the northern side of the square, just opposite the Town Hall, stands the Maison du Roi (House of the King), which was restored by Charles V but was never lived in by him nor by any other king. The rebuilt neo-Gothic version of the 19th century is no masterpiece, but its **Musée Communal** (Municipal Museum) deserves a visit. You will see some splendid stone sculptures, including the 14th- and 15th-century originals of the prophets, monks, torture victim and Moor preserved from the façade of the Town Hall. There is also an interesting selection of Brussels tapestries and some exquisite

*F*lower markets bring splashes of colour to the Grand-Place.

18th-century ceramics from the time when Brussels was a serious rival to Delft.

However, the top floor attracts the largest crowds. Here is the Manneken-Pis room displaying his wardrobe of more than 500 costumes, offered by countless visitors from all over the world, including made-to-measure, richly ornamented uniforms of African chiefs, Japanese samurai, British grenadiers and American cowboys.

Next to the Maison du Roi, from No. 28 to No. 24, are **La Chambrette de l'Amman**, (The House of the Amman) the duke's representative on the town council in the Middle Ages; **Le Pigeon**, once home to Victor Hugo and originally known as the House of the Painters – typically, the improverished artists could not afford to rebuild after the bombardment; and **La Chaloupe d'Or** (The Golden Longboat), the House of the Tailors.

On the eastern side of the square is the very impressive Flemish-Italian-style **Maison des Ducs de Brabant** (House of the Dukes of Brabant), **33**

Competition is so tough off the Grand-Place that it can be difficult to win an audience.

which is named after the statues on the façade's columns rather than the building's owners, who were in fact another group of old corporations.

The first of the three houses that brings us back round to the Town Hall, **L'Arbre d'Or** (The Golden Tree), No. 10, is the House of the Brewers, with its columns decorated with ears of wheat and hops' leaves, used in brewing the renowned Belgian beer. Inside, you can visit a genuine brewery transported here from Hoegaerden together with its forge; you will even be given the chance to sample a drop or two.

Next door is **Le Cygne** (The Swan). Now a restaurant, it once housed the butchers' corporation, and then a tavern where Karl Marx and Friedrich Engels hatched some of their revolutionary ideas propounded in their *Communist Manifesto* of 1848, and where the Belgian Workers' Party was founded in 1885.

Finally we arrive at **L'Etoile** (The Star), where the Amman stood at the balcony to witness beheadings. In an arcade at the side is a bas-relief of Everard't Serclaes, a 14th-century alderman who is shown dying of wounds inflicted by the Lord of Brasbant's henchmen for defending his city's interests. Like thousands before you, rub his arm and the nose of his dog for good luck.

34

Around the Grand-Place

The area immediately north of the Grand-Place has been designated **L'Ilot Sacré** (The Sacred Isle). Its name is a veritable cry from the heart of the municipality which finally decided to stand fast against the encroachments of property developers, who have done far more harm in recent times to historic Brussels than any foreign bombs or cannonballs.

Some of the tiny backstreets between the Rue du Marché aux Herbes and the Rue des Bouchers have been closed off to traffic. A number of the old houses are now restaurants – some with restored Renaissance gables, others retaining their ceramic, coloured-tile and stucco façades from the Belle Epoque at the turn of the 20th century. During the summer the streets are often enlivened with a variety of strolling musicians, acrobats, curiosity vendors and flower-sellers.

In the Rue de l'Ecuyer you will find the grand entrance to

Underground Art

The Brussels métro provides transport – and more. Art has gone underground, transforming tunnels and commuter platforms. All the works on display are by famous Belgian artists. The Bourse station features a revolving ceiling sculpture by Pol Bury and a dream-like painting of tram passengers by the great surrealist Paul Delvaux. At Comte de Flandre, 16 soaring bronze figures by Paul Van Hoeydonck, titled *16 x Icarus*, invade the tunnel. The urgent rhythms of Roger Somville's *Notre Temps* pulsate just above the tracks at Hankar, while ceramic tile designs by Jo Delahaut and Jean-Michel Folon's *Magic City* decorate Montgomery station.

The Société des Transports Intercommunaux de Bruxelles publishes a brochure describing the art in the métro, with several suggested itineraries to follow.

*D*elicate pastries and exquisite lace; you'll be tempted by the elegant shops of Brussels.

the **Galeries Saint-Hubert**, an attractive complex of glass-vaulted arcades housing restaurants and boutiques. It is the Galerie du Roi as far as the Rue des Bouchers, with the Galerie des Princes as a 'side-street' and the Galerie de la Reine continuing to the Rue du Marché aux Herbes. The arcades were pioneered in 1847 by Jean-Pierre Cluysenaar and their success among the boomingly prosperous bourgeoisie brought quite a few commissions from Milan and Paris. The interlocking galleries have a great advantage in this inner district, where so many of the tiny streets are impasses. Built originally as fire breaks, they increased in number as householders up to the 19th century extended their buildings backwards without reference to any overall plan. It may be quaint to look at, but it's tiresomely impractical for merchants.

Your walk around the Ilot Sacré will take you to the neo-classical **Théâtre de la Monnaie**, the opera house where the first rumbles of a revolution took place in 1830, leading consequently to national independence. North of the theatre is the bustling **Place de Brouckère** and the large shopping streets, Rue Neuve and Boulevard Anspach, on the arteries linking the two major railway stations, Gare du Nord and Gare du Midi – all surrounded by bold and uncompromising skyscrapers.

Hendrik Verbruggen's **pulpit** (1699) is a typically luxuriant baroque affair depicting Adam and Eve fleeing from the Garden of Eden.

The cathedral's artistic masterpiece, situated on the left of the choir, is the **Chapelle du Saint-Sacrement**, also closed for restoration work. Completed in 1539, it commemorates a 'miracle' of 1370, when Jews were alleged to have stolen the sacraments and stabbed them in ritual defilement, causing blood to spurt from the sacrament's 'wounds'. As a consequence, four Jewish families were burned at the stake.

Hopefully this background won't prevent you from admiring the magnificent **stained-glass windows** and **tapestries** depicting the story by Bernard van Orley and his pupils. Take a look too at the tombs, including those of various important historical figures of Brussels.

The magnificent stained-glass windows in the city's cathedral date from the 16th century.

Le Sablon

When you want to retreat from 20th-century Brussels, head for the Sablon area, south of the Grand-Place. Though perhaps the most elegant district of 19th-century Brussels, the Sablon ('sandy wasteland') was originally inhabited only by a hermit – and its marshes provided a burial ground for the overflow from the St-Jean hospital. These grim beginnings were forgotten when the guild of cross-bowmen built the chapel of Notre-Dame in 1304. The Sablon's glory was secured by the transfer of a healing statue of the Virgin Mary from Antwerp, drawing pilgrims from far and wide.

The **Place du Grand Sablon** is graced by restaurants in finely restored 17th- and 18th-century houses, antique shops and a weekend antiques market. The square forms a harmonious ensemble with the west side of the church. Notice the shape of the old Roman church design in the pavement.

On the south side, the pretty **Place du Petit Sablon** offers **39**

*A*fter a hard morning sight-seeing, relax in one of well-groomed
40 Brussels' many parks and gardens; here the Square du Petit Sablon.

Knocking off the Bird

Notre-Dame du Sablon was historically as much a focus of festivity as a place of worship. In 1530 Margarete of Austria organized a procession there to celebrate delivery from a plague and the festivities quickly turned into Brussels' annual July funfair. In 1615 the Archduchess Isabella delighted the crossbowmen by shooting down the bird emblem of their *Grand Serment* (Great Oath) from the steeple of the church. The crack markswoman was carried shoulder high through the streets and Brussels took the next three days off to celebrate.

a peaceful Renaissance-style garden and is filled with 19th-century bronze statues. Foremost among these are the great martyrs of Belgium, Counts Egmont and Hoorn. The Egmonts were one of the many aristocratic families who made the Sablon their home in the 16th century. It was the centre of a fashionable and cosmopolitan capital when the grand Austro-Spanish court enjoyed its heyday under Archduke Albert and Archduchess Isabella.

The restored **Palais d'Egmont** at the southern end of the square has been surrounded by many political controversies during its long history, including the one engendered by the all-important signature there which heralded Britain's entry into the (then called) European Common Market.

The church of **Notre-Dame du Sablon**, a masterpiece of Belgian Gothic architecture, took on its present shape in the early 15th century. Enter the church on the south side and take a look at the elegant porch crowned by fine rose-shaped stonework. The interior boasts a marvellous 17th-century baroque **pulpit**, with cherubim, angels and saints finely carved by Marcus De Vos. The pulpit proper is supported by a vigorous sculpture of the evangelical symbols of Mark, Luke, Matthew and John. On the left side of the choir, the sacrarium contains a notable *Adoration* **41**

Les Marolles

Moving slightly to the west, the city's other Gothic church of note is the **Notre-Dame de la Chapelle** at the fork of the Rue Haute and Rue Blaes at the north end of the popular quarter known as Les Marolles. This is the most appropriate last resting place of the great populist painter, Pieter Brueghel (c. 1520-1529). His marble mausoleum is marked by a sad story all too illustrative of the human frailty he loved to depict. At the request of Brueghel's son, Rubens painted a picture in tribute to the great master, *Christ Handing the Keys to St Peter*, but the church decided to sell the painting in 1765 and unfortunately, it now has only a copy.

It seems highly probable that Pieter Brueghel lived and died just down the street from the church, at 132 Rue Haute. At any rate, it's a fine old gabled **house** which has been restored (some argue, not entirely faithfully) in the beamed style of the period (1563-69). Above all, the

*T*he church of Notre-Dame du Sablon boasts some fine examples of ornate baroque carving.

of the Magi. Next to that is the chapel of the family of Thurn and Tassis, nobles who began the first European postal service in Brussels in the 16th century. In stark black marble, it contrasts with the white statuary of Lucas Fayd'herbe.

neighbourhood itself, Les Marolles, around the Rue Haute and the Rue Blaes, is delightful, with its busy street life centred on an old working-class district where the city historically kept its sense of humour whenever the rest of the town was falling apart. Linguists will appreciate the rich dialect mixing Flemish, French, Spanish and smatterings of Italian, German and Hebrew – a perfect inventory of the invaders and refugees who have passed through over the centuries.

The names of the numerous streets bunched between the Rue Blaes and Rue Haute bear testimony to the fact that this is above all a working neighbourhood – Rue des Orfèvres (goldsmiths), des Ramoneurs (chimney-sweeps), des Charpentiers (carpenters), des Brodeurs (embroiderers), Rue des Tonneliers (coopers), and Rue des Chaisiers (chair-makers). The corporations actually used to gather around the Grand-Place, and the names are a 1920s tribute to the trades rather than an indication of where their workshops could be found.

At the southern end of Les Marolles, take a good look at the **Porte de Hal**, last vestige of the city's medieval fortified ramparts. This grand gate was built in the 14th century, soon after the Count of Flanders was driven away. The huge façade facing the city centre is a 19th-century addition, as is the staircase which gave the building its horse-shoe shape. These changes were carried out in order to house the Museum of Folklore, which it still does today.

Coming back towards the centre, it's difficult to miss the huge **Palais de Justice**, the biggest building constructed in the 19th century. Altogether, it covers over 2½ ha (6½ acres), including the spot where most common criminals were hanged (the uncommon ones were kept for the Grand-Place or the Grand Sablon). The long years of its construction (1866-83) spanned the period of Belgium's spectacular economic, industrial and imperial growth, and the huge, sprawling, soaring neo-Greco-Roman and Assyrian structure is the bombastic epitome of its age. In order to build the Palais de Justice, it was necessary to raze to the ground a large part of Les Marolles and to this day the word 'architect' in the Brussels dialect has pejorative overtones.

The splendid Rue de la Régence leads from the Palais de Justice to the Place Royale and the **Palais du Roi**, the official place of business of the king of the Belgians. Built in the 18th century on the site of the old court of Brussels, it is open to the public from the end of July to the beginning of September.

Museums

Now for the main attractions of the Place Royale: the **Musées Royaux des Beaux Arts de Belgique**, where the creative genius of the Low Countries is unquestionable. The museums are divided into the Musée d'Art Ancien (up to the mid-19th century) and the Musée d'Art Moderne (late 19th and 20th centuries). Behind

them is the grand Bibliothèque Royale (Royal Library).

The **Musée d'Art Ancien** was established in 1801 as a huge depository for whatever the French revolutionary armies could not carry back to Paris. Soon after Waterloo, the greater part of the plunder was recuperated, and the collection now consists of some 1,200 paintings, most of them from the great old Flemish schools. Pride of place goes to Brueghel and Rubens, but it is well worth lingering over a few of the other masters of the Low Countries, who are both subtle and robust in style.

Begin with the Master of Flémalle, Robert Campin, an early 15th-century teacher of the more celebrated Roger van der Weyden. His *Annunciation* shows the angel revealing to Mary her divine destiny in the charming setting of a Flemish bourgeois home.

Unfortunately, most of the best work of **Roger van der Weyden** (c.1399-1464), Brussels' official municipal painter, was destroyed by Louis XIV's bombardment in 1695, but his

MUSEUMS and ART GALLERIES

Centre belge de la bande dessinée (Belgian Comic Strip Centre), *The Waucquez Warehouse, 20 rue des Sables, 1000 Brussels*. History of the comic strip in Belgium. Open Tue-Sun 10am-6pm; BF150. Métro: Botanique, Gare Centrale. Tram: 52, 58, 81, 90. Bus: 38, 58, 61. Disabled access. (See p.49)

Hôtel de Ville (Town Hall), *Grand-Place, 1000 Brussels*. Sculptures, Brussels tapestries, Gothic woodwork and paintings. Open: (Oct-Mar) Tue-Fri 9.30am-12.15pm and 1.45-4pm; (Apr-Sep) 1.45-5pm; Sunday and public holidays 10am-noon and 2-4pm; BF75. Guided tours only. Métro: Bourse, Gare Centrale. Tram: 52, 55, 81. Bus: 34, 48, 95, 96. (See p.28)

Musée d'Art Ancien (Museum of Fine Arts), *3 rue de la Régence, 1000 Brussels*. Art from the 15th to 19th century; access to Musée d'Art Moderne. Open Tue-Sun 10am-noon and 1-5pm; Free. Métro: Gare Centrale, Parc. Tram: 92, 93, 94. Bus: 95, 96. Disabled access. (See p.44)

Musée d'Art Moderne (Museum of Modern Art), *1-2 pl. Royale, 1000 Brussels*. 20th-century art; access to Musée d'Art Ancien. Open Tue-Sun 10am-1pm and 2-5pm; Free. Métro: Gare Centrale, Parc. Tram: 92, 93, 94. Bus: 95, 96. Disabled access. (See p.48)

Musée Horta (Horta Museum), *25 rue Américaine, 1060 Brussels*. In art nouveau house of Victor Horta. Open Tue-Sun 2-5.30pm; BF100, (weekend) BF200. Tram: 81, 82, 91, 92. (See p.49)

Musée Instrumental (Instrument Museum of the Royal Music Conservatory), *17 Petit Sablon, 1000 Brussels*. International instrument display. Open Tue-Sat 2.30-4.30pm; Sun 10.30am-12.30pm; Free. Tram: 92, 93, 94. Bus: 95, 96. Disabled access. (See p.48)

Musée Royal de l'Armée et d'Histoire Militaire (Royal Museum of the Army and Military History), *Parc du Cinquantenaire, 3, 1040 Brussels*. One of the largest museums of military history in the world. Open Tue-Sun 9am-noon and 1-4.45pm; Free. Métro: Mérode, Schuman. Tram: 20, 61, 80. Disabled access. (See p.52)

Musées Royaux d'Art et d'Histoire (Royal Art and History Museum), *10 Parc du Cinquantenaire, 1040 Brussels*. Antiquity, non-European cultures, Belgian archaeology. Open Tue-Fri 9.30am-5pm; weekends and holidays 10am-5pm; Free. Métro: Mérode, Schuman. Tram: 20, 61, 80, 81. Disabled access. (See p.52)

sorrowful *Pietà* and expressive *Man with an Arrow* remain as fine examples of his style.

One of the highlights of the Brussels' art collection is *The Judgement of Emperor Otto* by **Dirk Bouts** (c.1415-75). The

*E*njoy the fine neo-classical façade of the Musées Royaux des Beaux Arts de Belgique.

diptych relates the episode in which Otto was duped by his wife into beheading an innocent man (*Punishment of the Innocent*) and then recognized his dreadful mistake when the widow faced the *Ordeal by Fire*. The consummate control of the Dutch painter captures these horrible events with true beauty and reserve.

You will notice something of the same detachment in *The Martyrdom of St Sebastian* by **Hans Memling** (c.1435-94), where the precise skills of the archers are given as much emphasis as the terrible suffering of Sebastian.

Because many paintings by **Hieronymus Bosch** (c.1450-1516) seem full of menace and strange surrealism, the rather conventional *Crucifixion* here may come as a surprise. All the same, Bosch couldn't resist throwing in the black raven of death on the left above a skull and the bones of previous crucifixion victims.

Pieter Brueghel (c.1525-69) is very well represented here. *The Fall of Icarus* is the perfect epitome of the great master's mixture of serenity and cynicism, showing peasants going about their work while poor Icarus falls into the sea, a literal illustration of the old Flemish proverb that 'no plough stops for a dying man'. Brueghel's acute social observation in *The Census at Bethlehem* transposes the census taking in the Palestine desert to tax collection in the snows of Flanders. In another winter scene, *Skaters and Bird Trap*, the picture's fragile tranquillity is threatened by the impression that the skaters might at any moment fall through the ice and the birds topple the trap that is over their heads.

Peter Paul Rubens (1577-1640) is also displayed here in strength. You should look especially for his unusual studies of *Negro Heads*, and you will find the smiling face reproduced in one of the three Magi in *The Adoration of the Magi*. Two more characteristically exuberant Rubenesque Rubens are *The Way of the Cross*, which makes the final climb to Calvary more triumphant than tragic, and the extremely fero-

*A*rt appreciation can be hard work; take the time to enjoy Brussels' great collections.

cious *Martyrdom of St Livinius*. In this rather gruesome painting, a magnificent scarlet-hatted bandit has just torn out the poor bishop's tongue with a pair of pincers.

Calm yourself with the restfully domestic *Portrait of a Genoese Lady and her Daughter* by **Anthony van Dyck** (1599-1641) and **Frans Hals'** (1580-1666) charming *Group of Children*. **47**

The German painter **Lucas Cranach** (1472-1553) is represented here by a solemn portrait of *Dr Scheyring,* as well as a mischievous-looking *Eve* and innocent *Adam.*

Rembrandt (1606-69) is not very well represented in Brussels, but his portrait of *Nicolaas van Bambeeck* definitely deserves your attention.

To give you a better idea of what the Spanish were like when they ruled Brussels, take a close look at the painting of *Apollo Flaying Marsyas* by José de Ribera (c.1591-1652). Apollo is pictured calmly skinning Marsyas alive. Look, too for another well-known death scene: David's *Marat Assassinated in his Bathtub.*

Later art tends to favour the French and includes works by Courbet, Sisley and Delacroix.

A passageway takes you to the refurbished, subterranean **Musée d'Art Moderne**, also accessible via Place Royale. Among the Belgian masters on display here are Rik Wouters, René Magritte and Paul Delvaux, each taking a pot-shot at **48** the bourgeoisie from a vari-ously erotic, satiric, or surreal point of view. A few foreign moderns are also here from Matisse to Henry Moore. On show in the entrance hall is work by Richard Lang.

Among the city's other museums, you should visit the **Musées Royaux d'Art et d'Histoire** in the south-east corner of the Parc du Cinquantenaire. Here you will find a whole panorama of world civilization. The collections range from the ancient arts of Mesopotamia, Egypt, Iran, Greece and Rome to Oriental masterpieces of Japan, China, Korea, Cambodia and India. You will also find pre-Columbian sculpture of the Mayans and Aztecs from Mexico and Peru; Brussels and Tournai tapestries, Delft china and Brussels lace; plus a marvellous collection of 18th-century carriages, coaches, sleighs and sedan-chairs in the Musée de la Voiture.

*T*he Belgian Comic Strip Centre houses a vast library including over 25,000 comic albums!

Music-lovers will enjoy the **Musée Instrumental** on the Rue de la Régence next to the Conservatoire. The collection of 6000 pieces (of which 500 are on display) includes rare 16th to 18th century instruments. The **Centre belge de la bande dessinée** (Belgian Comic Strip Centre) offers exhibitions as well as the world's largest comic book library. The museum is housed on the Rue des Sables in an Art Nouveau building designed by Victor Horta.

Brussels was home to several influential **Art Nouveau** architects, notably Victor Horta, Paul Hankar and Henry Van de Velde. Two houses built in 1893 by Horta and Hankar launched the movement here: Horta's Hôtel Tassel (6 Rue P.-E. Janson) and Hankar's house at 71 Rue Defacqz. Strongly inspired by nature, their styles marked the two main tendencies in Brussels Art Nouveau. The **Musée Horta** (23–25 rue Américaine) is full of local treasures of this period. The

typical curved lines, windows, mirrors, staircase, woodwork and wrought iron of the house itself show how a new decorative dimension was given to the most utilitarian of objects. Guided tours of Art Nouveau buildings in Brussels are held by ARAU (tel. 513 4761). The Tourist and Information Office of Brussels can also provide details (see p.137).

Peripheral Attractions

As well as containing one of Horta's houses at number 224, the **Avenue Louise** can claim to be the city's most elegant shopping street. It's also worth taking time to wander through the gracious residential neighbourhoods found around the smart **Square Marie-Louise** and **Ambiorix** in the St Josse district (Art Nouveau Maison St Cyr is at 11 Square Ambiorix and the Hôtel Van Eetvelde is at 2 Avenue Palmerston). In contrast, you can see striking modern architecture, such as the round Glaverbel building, in the Boulevard du Souverain and the Chaussée de la Hulpe.

Following Avenue Louise south, you will pass the Cistercian **Abbaye de la Cambre** in Ixelles, originally dating from 1196 and rebuilt in the 1930s. The stained glass, statuary and paintings found inside the

A quiet moment among the fountains of the Parc de Bruxelles.

14th-century church are mostly modern in origin, but there is a fine head of Christ by the 15th-century artist, Albert Bouts.

One of the illustrious men of the Renaissance, the great humanist Erasmus, lived for a brief period in Brussels. Dating from 1515, the **House of Erasmus**, in the borough of Anderlecht (Rue du Chapitre), has been turned into a fascinating museum of the philosopher's career, with paintings, original letters and manuscripts exchanged with the great men of his time. The house is also worth a visit for its own particular charm. The fine Gothic structure has Renaissance additions around the courtyard, a harmonious ensemble of Dutch and Spanish styles. While you're in Anderlecht, take a quick look at the **Béguinage** (at the end of the Rue du Chapelain), a 16th-century nunnery where eight nuns lived and worked at the budding lace industry.

Parc des Expositions, where Brussels held its World Fair in 1958, is the site of the **Atomi-**

The Atomium – the city's most spectacular landmark.

um, a hugely magnified iron crystal molecule. Let Europe's fastest lift take you, at 5m per second, to the top, where there is a restaurant and a spectacular view of the city. At the bottom there are exhibitions on scientific themes. Nearby is **Bruparck**, an amusement centre containing 'mini-Europe', an exhibition of scale-models of famous European buildings. For film buffs, the Kinepolis in Bruparck is the largest cinema complex in the world, with 26 screens and an Imax theatre with a $600m^2$ ($6,456ft^2$) screen for a spectacular experience. **51**

... and Parks

Brussels is also a city of magnificent parks. One of them lies in the very heart of the city, the **Parc de Bruxelles**, off the Rue Royale between the Palais du Roi and Palais de la Nation. It has a special place in the capital's history, for it was there that the Dutch army was hemmed in by the Belgian revolutionary militia during the victorious fight for independence in September 1830. Today, you can relax amidst its graceful baroque statues.

Just east of the Rond-Point Schuman, where the European Union has its headquarters, is the **Parc du Cinquantenaire**. It was laid out in 1880 to celebrate Belgium's 50th anniversary of independence and is now the largest museum complex in Belgium, comprising among others the Musées Royaux d'Art et d'Histoire; the Musée Royal de l'Armée et d'Histoire Militaire; and **Autoworld**, one of the world's biggest collections of vintage cars. Continuing along the Avenue de Tervuren, you will reach the **Parc de Woluwe**, bordering on the 'beaux quartiers' of the south east.

Lovers of botanical gardens flock every spring to the park at the **Domaine Royal de Laeken**, a playground for the Spanish and Austrian nobility in the 16th and 17th centuries. At the top end of the Avenue du Parc Royal are the royal greenhouses (*serres Royales*). The tropical plants can be viewed by the public (see p.29) and are illuminated at night during May. Nearby is a rare Chinese pavilion and the highest Japanese pagoda in Europe.

The citizens' favourite park remains the **Bois de la Cambre** at the far end of the Avenue Louise, just a 15-minute tram or bus ride from the Palais de Justice. Known simply as the 'Bois' (wood), amid long groves of beech trees and boating lakes, it's the perfect place to rest aching feet.

The Bois de la Cambre is only the municipal tip of the **Forêt de Soignes**, Europe's largest beech forest, which extends over to the **Parc de Tervuren** thus forming a massive

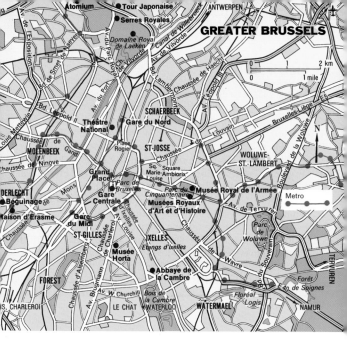

GREATER BRUSSELS

curtain of dense green forest and rolling parkland across the south-east corner of Brussels. This was where Charles V and his aunt Margarete of Austria and sister Maria of Hungary loved to go hunting, in an area that is today the districts of Le Logis and Floréal. There is a superb Arboretum at Tervuren and the forest has splendid lakes (such as Lac de Genval) for boating and watersports.

For a change of pace, visit the fascinating **Musée Royal de l'Afrique Centrale** for its huge collection of African art, ethnology and natural history. At the far end of the forest is the **Château de Rixensart**, a vast red-brick Renaissance pile belonging to the Princes de Merode. There is a cloister-like courtyard and the interior is richly furnished in Louis XV and Louis XVI style.

Excursions

All the places suggested here can be reached in a couple of hours by road or rail from Brussels. Waterloo is closest, an 18km (12 mile) drive south on the N5, or a short train ride (Brussels-Charleroi line) or a bus trip away. For the other destinations, a logical itinerary would be to start off with Antwerp, 46km (29 miles) to the north, then head west 60km (37 miles) to take in Ghent and 49km (30 miles) Bruges, from which it's just a short hop 27km (17 miles) to Ostend and other resorts on the coast. Any of these places can be seen on a day's outing from Brussels, or combined with a more extensive tour of Flanders.

WATERLOO

History buffs will need no encouragement to make this trip out of Brussels. In fact, few people with the curiosity to come to Belgium in the first place will want to miss this landmark in European history, the site of the battle that ended Napoleon's empire. There is something extraordinarily moving about standing amid the peaceful farmlands and imagining the tumult and bloodshed of 18 June 1815. The fighting left around 11,000 dead and wounded some 35,000 British, Dutch, Prussian, French, and Belgian soldiers.

The town of Waterloo itself, 5km (3 miles) north of the battlefield, has a **Wellington Museum** in the house where the British general set up his headquarters on the eve of battle. The museum includes battle plans and letters, maps, and has the original furniture in Wellington's bedroom.

South of the battlefield, at Vieux-Genappe, is the **Ferme du Caillou**, the farm where Napoleon once had his headquarters. In more recent times it has been transformed into a museum, with the great man's camp-bed, hat and utensils.

The **Butte du Lion** (easily visible to the west of the N5) is a striking monument to commemorate the battle, erected by the Dutch on the spot where the Prince of Orange was wounded. The 40½m (133ft) mound is topped with a cast-iron lion looking in the direction of France, and gives a fine overall view of the battlefield. Legend erroneously has it that the lion is made of cannons and cannonballs.

Climb up the mound's 226 steps to see the various positions taken across the battlefield by the opposing armies. But remember that everything from up there looks deceptively flat. You can't appreciate the hazards and advantages of each military formation until you walk all around the field itself, seeing it from the soldier's point of view. Each dip and slightest rise in the ground made the difference between life and death.

At the base of the mound is an interesting museum with a painted panorama of the battlefield and an audiovisual account of the fighting. In the inevitable souvenir shop, you may be interested to see that busts of the defeated Napoleon outnumber those of the winners Wellington and Blücher about 500 to one.

This monument pays special tribute to the Prince of Orange at the site where he was wounded.

Arm yourself with an illustrated guide to the battlefield and a pair of binoculars to appreciate the strategic importance of such redoubts as the farms of Hougoumont, Papelotte and La Haie-Sainte where the fiercest pitched battles actually took place. Try to visit **Hougoumont**, south west of the Butte du Lion, where the walls of the farmyard bear a **55** modest plaque of the British Coldstream Guards, who in 1944 helped liberate Belgium, in honour of their fallen comrades of Waterloo.

Standing at the northern end of the battlefield, at Wellington's position above **La Haie-Sainte**, you can appreciate his enormous advantage, with infantry concealed behind a crest at his back, looking down on the exposed French armies all around La Belle-Alliance 2km (1¼ miles) to the south. Napoleon's soldiers were better disciplined and experienced and the battle was very close. It was only the arrival of Blücher's Prussian troops from Wavre that tipped the balance. **La Belle-Alliance**, the farm where Blücher and Wellington met to congratulate each other afterwards, stands to this day.

ANTWERP

Population 750,000

Although it never held the status of a capital in the political life of the Low Countries, the economic and cultural prominence of Antwerp (*Antwerpen/Anvers*) made it for a long period perhaps the most important town in northern Europe, the north pole of a whole flourishing trading and artistic axis that included Florence, Venice and Genoa.

The peak of its power came during the 15th century, when Bruges' access to the sea silted up and Antwerp's Schelde River was widened by flooding. Thereafter, Antwerp became the principal port of the Low Countries. Its dominant position continued well into the 16th century as a clearing-house for all the new riches – spices, silks, gold and precious stones – brought back by the Portuguese from the Indies.

This was the town to which Peter Paul Rubens was proud to return and make his home during the most glorious years of his life, and the town where Christophe Plantin created Europe's greatest printing plant.

Today the port is booming again, rivalling Rotterdam and Hamburg as a gateway for Europe's imports and exports. Antwerp has also become the largest diamond-cutting centre for the world market. The town's prosperity has enabled it, despite the devastations of World War II, to preserve and restore the magnificent monuments of its past – a marvellous cathedral, a *grand-place* to match that of the capital, Rubens' fine residence, and rich collections of art. These, along with its bustling port life, make Antwerp a truly delightful one-day excursion, with the calculated risk that you might well end up staying longer than you planned.

Approach the vast cathedral across the triangular **Handschoenmarkt** (glove market) with its ornate well which is attributed to Quentin Metsys (c.1466-1531), a leading Flemish portrait painter. The statue up above is of the town's legendary hero, Silvius Brabo. Nearby is situated the Torengebouw which, when built in 1930, stood at 87m (285ft) and was Europe's first sky-scraper.

 The **Kathedraal** (*Onze Lieve Vrouw*), with the creamy white tones of its masonry, is a wonderful 14th- and 15th-century Gothic edifice. Like so many other churches of that era, it resembles a mother hen with an assortment of houses built onto its walls. Though architectural purists sometimes complain that they conceal important elements of the cathedral's exterior design, this is more than compensated for by the powerful impression of a church inexorably integrated into its parish.

The beauty of the cathedral derives above all from the majestic purity of its open stonework **steeple**, at 120m (400ft) high it rises over the octagonal dome at the other end of the building. The spacious interior also conveys the essential nobility of the cathedral, a feeling reinforced by the **Rubens masterpieces** that decorate it. His works include a triptych in the right transept showing the descent of Christ's body from the cross; the altarpiece in the choir is a glowing *Assumption*; and the titanic *Raising of the Cross* found in the left transept, was painted in 1610 just after Rubens returned from his trip to Italy full of Rome's Renaissance splendour.

57

The largest of all the cathedral's ten chapels is St Anthony's, with its beautiful 1503 stained-glass window showing King Henry VII of England kneeling down with his queen. The window commemorated, appropriately enough for mercantile Antwerp, a commercial treaty between England and the Low Countries.

Just south of the cathedral is **Groenplaats** (Green Square), which was once the cathedral cemetery. Today it is a lively square with open-air cafés bordering a charming, tree-shaded centre with a statue of Rubens.

As in Brussels, Antwerp's **Grote Markt** (Grand-Place) emphasizes the primordial role that the burghers of the self-assertive corporations played in the city's history. The **Stadhuis** (Town Hall) is a shining monument of municipal pride, a towering structure embodying Antwerp's historic position linking both northern and southern Europe, as well as combining Italian Renaissance columns with Gothic lattice-windows and gables quite typical of the Low Countries.

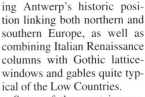

Some of the most impressive **corporation houses** are No. 3, De Witte Engel (House of the White Angel); No. 5, Het Kuiperhuis (House of the Coopers); No. 7, finest of them all, De Oude Voetboog (House of the Old Crossbow); and No. 11, Meerseniershuis (House of the Haberdashers). All have been restored in 16th-century Flemish Renaissance style.

The Brabo fountain (19th-century) on Grote Markt was designed by Jef Lambeaux. Silvius Brabo is said to have cut off an evil giant's hand and thrown it away, thus making the whole town safe from tyranny and giving it its name – *hand werpen* (hand-throw).

*L*ighting up time for Antwerp's Grote Markt, watched over by the fountain of Silvius Brabo. **59**

Rubenshuis (Rubensstraat 9-11, off the main street of the Meir) offers ample proof that Rubens hardly fits the conventional view of a famous but impoverished artist. He made a lot of money painting for the greatest monarchs of Europe and built himself a wonderful house in 1610 when he came to Antwerp to spend the last 30 years of his life.

As a residence for his family of eight children by his two wives, Isabella Brant and Hélène Fourment, the entire left wing of the house was, in traditional Flemish style, quite austerely furnished, but the tastes Rubens acquired in Italy were given free rein when it came to equipping his studio in the right wing. This opulently baroque side of the building also served as a museum for his vast personal collection of ancient Greek and Roman sculpture and Flemish and Italian paintings, much of which is still on display. The collection contains paintings by Jan Brueghel, Snyders, Jordaens and Veronese, as well as several of his own paintings, including a self-portrait which is displayed in the dining-room.

The late-Gothic church of **Sint Jacobskerk** (east of the cathedral) has splendid art on view inside, especially in the **Rubens Chapel** behind the choir where the artist and his family are buried. The painting just over the altar is one of the master's last works, in which, so experts say, he has depicted his two wives as the Madonna and Mary Magdalen, and himself as Saint George.

One of the most fascinating windows on Antwerp's golden age of the 16th century is the **Plantin-Moretus Museum** (in Vrijdagmarkt 22). It is the fine Renaissance house of Christophe Plantin, still considered to be one of the most important craftsmen-businessmen of the Spanish Empire's heyday. Plantin's house and the printing presses housed next door present a marvellous history of

Rubens' Femme au Perroquet from Antwerp's extensive collection of Flemish art.

printing, books and the evolution of handwriting itself. Just seven of the original 22 printing presses have been kept in perfect working order and the museum will even run off a copy of a sonnet by Plantin as a souvenir. The most precious exhibit of the collection is the revered **Biblia Regia**, or Polyglot Bible, printed in 1568-72 in a staggering eight volumes, in Hebrew, Syriac, Aramaic, Latin and Greek. The foreign collection also includes one of the best surviving Gutenberg Bibles from 1455 and a very rare copy of the Papal Index of forbidden books dating from around 1569. Rubens has, as usual, obliged with some fine family portraits.

The **Koninklijk Museum voor Schone Kunsten** (Musée royal des Beaux-Arts) has an excellent collection of Flemish art housed in a tastefully modernized building. Pride of place is naturally given to Rubens, with magnificent versions of the *Adoration of the Magi* and *St Francis of Assisi*, but his followers van Dyck and Jordaens are also well represented. Among the earlier works to look out for: a portrait of Jean de Candida by

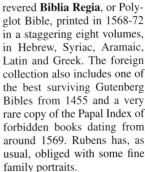

*T*he port of Antwerp and its history are explored in the National Maritime Museum.

Hans Memling; an altar triptych by Roger van der Weyden depicting the *Seven Sacraments*; *The Honest Judges* and *The Holy Women* by Dirk Bouts; and two works by another Antwerp master, Quentin Massys, *Mary Magdalen* and *The Burial of Christ*.

Visiting the modern collection you can admire Belgium's contribution to the surreal vision of our times, which was prefigured by James Ensor at the turn of the century and brought to fruition by René Magritte and Paul Delvaux in the 1930s. Foreign artists include Lovis Corinth, Rodin, Modigliani and Zadkine.

If Brussels whetted your appetite for Pieter Brueghel, then try and visit the **Mayer van den Bergh Museum** (at the corner of Lange Gasthuisstraat and Arenbergstraat). Here you can see the artist's vehemently pessimistic vision of war, *Dulle Griet* (Angry Maggie, see p.85), and his earliest known signed work, the *Twelve Proverbs*. Some of the other highlights include a lovely *Virgin and Child* by van der Weyden

and a *Crucifixion* triptych by Quentin Massys.

Antwerp possesses one of Europe's most important **Zoological Gardens** (*Dierentuin*), which is behind the Central Railway Station – a masterpiece in its own right. Every effort is made to give the animals as much freedom and as normal an environment as possible. The gorillas and orangoutangs are outstanding, as are the rare white rhinos. The zoo's most striking feature is perhaps the innovative system of the bird's cages-without-cages. Exotic birds are able to fly freely among the trees and foliage without coming into contact with the public – or escaping – by an ingenious system of lighting that keeps the birds well illuminated and the spectators in total darkness.

For more trees and greenery, go south to **Nachtegalen** and **Middelheim parks**. The latter has a delightful open-air sculpture museum which includes pieces by Rodin, Henry Moore and Maillol.

Before visiting the port, if you want to appreciate the **63** historic and modern personality of Antwerp, then stop off at the **Nationaal Scheepvaart Museum** (Maritime Museum), which is housed in Antwerp's oldest building, a 16th-century castle known as the **Steen** built on the right bank of the River Schelde. The Maritime Museum will give you a keen sense of the importance of the sea in Antwerp's history, with its collections of old maritime maps, nautical instruments and seafaring paraphernalia, and the strange mysticism surrounding the figureheads which adorned the prows of ships plying the seas to make Antwerp's fortune. Children will enjoy the meticulous ship models and clever boats-in-a-bottle.

 Properly primed for the sea, you can take a tour around the busy **port** (*haven*) of Antwerp. The best way to see it is on one of the regular boat trips which leave from the Steen. They can last 50 minutes or up to three hours, depending on the degree of your passion for shipping. Try to go on a weekday when port activity is at its greatest along the 80km (50 miles) of quays and docks. As you move among the little cargo boats and monster oil tankers, you'll be able to get a close look at the work of loading and unloading the huge containers from the ships, repairing and refitting in one of 18 dry docks, as well as the operations of the six gigantic sluices linking the river with the docks. Antwerp claims that its port is 'the fastest in the world' at getting a ship in, unloading, reloading and getting it out to sea again. Your tour will show you all the sounds, movements and sometimes the somewhat pungent smells of this vital enterprise in Belgium's economy.

GHENT

Population 250,000

Ghent (*Gent* in Flemish and *Gand* in French) is a fiercely independent-minded Flemish municipality. The town made its mark in Belgian history in AD 610, when its pagan inhabitants threw the Christian missionary, St Amand, into the River Schelde.

A Selection of
Hotels and Restaurants
in and around Brussels

Recommended Hotels

Brussels has a large number of hotels to choose from – more than 100 in the city itself and others in the suburbs. The Tourist and Information Office of Brussels publishes its own hotel guide book which covers every price range. The selection below is based on price, location and general standard of facilities. As a basic guide we have used the symbols below to indicate the price per night for a double room with bath, including breakfast. Note that the lower priced hotels are sometimes older and smaller.

I	below BF4,000
II	BF4,000-6,000
III	above BF6,000

BRUSSELS

L'Agenda   II
6 rue Florence
1050 Brussels
Tel. 539 0031
Fax 539 0063
40 rooms. Simple but comfortable interior in this bed-and-breakfast-style hotel. Near Avenue Louise, it has the advantages of nearby public transport without the noise.

Amigo   III
1-3 rue de l'Amigo
1000 Brussels
Tel. 547 4747
Fax 513 5277
175 rooms. Beautifully furnished interior with traditional Flemish decor. Discretion and personalized service are the keynotes here.

Archimède   II
22 rue Archimède
1040 Brussels
Tel. 231 0909
Fax 230 3371
56 rooms. A hotel with a personal touch. Only 5 minutes from the nearest métro and the EU building. Mini-bar and laundry facilities are available; breakfast dining hall, but no restaurant.

Arenberg   II
15 rue d'Assaut
1000 Brussels
Tel. 511 0770
Fax 514 1976

155 rooms. A delightfully decorated hotel with all modern conveniences in addition to conference facilities, garage, parking, restaurant and bar. Very convenient location in the centre of town.

Ascot   ▯

1 place Loix
1060 Brussels
Tel. 538 8835
Fax 538 8835
60 rooms. This modern, comfortable and clean hotel is only 2 minutes' walk from the nearest métro station. No restaurant.

Bedford   ▯▯▯

135 rue Midi
1000 Brussels
Tel. 512 7840
Fax 514 1759
279 rooms. An English-style hotel with a rustic feel only 2 minutes away from the Grand-Place. Excellent facilities include a restaurant, bar and conference rooms.

Brussels Europa Hotel   ▯▯▯

107 rue de la Loi
1040 Brussels
Tel. 230 1333
Fax 230 0120
240 rooms. A beautifully decorated, luxurious high-rise hotel, with two restaurants, bar and parking.

Conrad Brussels   ▯▯▯

71 avenue Louise
1050 Brussels
Tel. 542 4242
Fax 542 4200
269 rooms. This luxury business hotel with its classic interior has a fitness centre, sauna, restaurant, conference rooms, disabled and parking facilities.

County House   ▯▯

2 square des Héros
1180 Brussels
Tel. 375 4420
Fax 375 3122
101 rooms. Close to the airport, this pleasant hotel is a 20-minute walk from the centre. Restaurant.

Euro-flat   ▯▯

50 boulevard Charlemagne
1040 Brussels
Tel. 230 0010
Fax 230 3683
133 rooms. Close to the EU headquarters, this hotel has a fitness room, sauna, laundry and parking facilities, and a breakfast room overlooking the garden.

Hilton International Brussels   ▯▯▯

38 boulevard Waterloo
1000 Brussels
Tel. 504 1111
Fax 504 2111

67

450 rooms. Luxury business hotel with a Maison du Boeuf restaurant and Plein-Ciel restaurant with excellent views over the city. Restaurant, music bar, sauna, disabled access, garage, conference rooms.

Holiday Inn Brussels Airport ▯▯▯
Holidaystraat 7
1831 Diegem
Tel. 720 5865
Fax 720 4145
In a good location at Brussels airport, this highly acclaimed hotel provides superb standards of comfort. Indoor pool and tennis court.

Ibis Bruxelles City Sainte-Catherine ▯
2 rue Joseph Plateau
1000 Brussels
Tel. 513 7620
Fax 514 2214
235 rooms. Bar, conference rooms and disabled facilities are available in this modern, comfortable hotel.

Ibis off Grand-Place ▯
100 Grasmarkt/rue du Marché-aux-Herbes
1000 Brussels
Tel 514 4040
Fax 514 5067
172 rooms. Situated in a handy location near the Grand-Place, this hotel has a bar, restaurant, conference rooms and disabled facilities.

Jolly Hotel Atlanta ▯▯
7 boulevard Adolphe-Max
1000 Brussels
Tel. 217 0120
Fax 217 3758
241 rooms. The top-floor restaurant offers great views over city. Music bar, conference facilities, disabled access and garage.

Le Dix-septième ▯
25 rue de la Madeleine
1000 Brussels
Tel. 502 5744
Fax 502 6424
17 rooms. Small, quiet hotel with antique furniture. Bar and sauna.

Léopold ▯
35 Luxemburgstraat
1040 Brussels
Tel. 511 1828
Fax 514 1939
86 rooms. Comfortable hotel with restaurant and bar, sauna, conference rooms, garden and parking.

Mayfair ▯▯▯
381-383 avenue Louise
1050 Brussels
Tel. 649 9800
Fax 649 2249
99 rooms. This hotel with its classic and traditional interior design

has its own restaurant and bar, conference rooms, laundry facilities and private garage.

Métropole   ▯▯▯

31 place de Brouckère
1000 Brussels
Tel. 217 2300
Fax 218 0220

410 rooms. This is a large, stylish and unique hotel which features art nouveau elegance in its interior design. Restaurant and music bar, fitness centre and sauna, disabled access and private parking.

Park Hotel   ▯▯

21-22 avenue de l'Yser
1040 Brussels
Tel. 735 7400
Fax 735 1967

51 rooms. This hotel has a wonderful garden, restaurant, sauna and conference facilities.

Président Nord   ▯▯

107 boulevard Adolphe-Max
1000 Brussels
Tel. 219 0060
Fax 218 1269

63 rooms. Situated only 10 minutes away from the busy Grand-Place and la Gare du Nord, this modern-style building is undergoing extensive interior renovation and decoration. Bar and dining room facilities available.

President World Trade Center   ▯▯

180 boulevard Emile Jacqmain
1210 Brussels
Tel. 203 2020
Fax 203 2440

310 rooms. This is a luxury hotel, conveniently situated for the Gare du Nord. Facilities include a well-equipped fitness centre, restaurant and music bar, sauna, conference facilities, garage, private parking and a garden.

Royal Crown Brussels   ▯▯▯

250 rue Royale
1210 Brussels
Tel. 220 6611
Fax 217 8444

315 rooms. A large hotel with a pleasing and comfortable rustic feel. Japanese- and English-style restaurants, all-day piano bar, conference rooms and garage.

Royal Windsor Hotel   ▯▯▯

5 rue Duquesnoy
1000 Brussels
Tel. 505 5555
Fax 511 6004

275 rooms. In an excellent location near the Business Grand-Place, this hotel has a restaurant and music bar, private club, conference facilities, a fitness centre and garage.

69

SAS Royal Hotel ▯▯▯
47 rue du Fossé-aux-Loups
1000 Brussels
Tel. 219 2828
Fax 219 7070
281 rooms in various styles. The lobby of this hotel houses a small section of the 12th-century city wall. Restaurant, music bar, fitness centre, sauna, disabled access and garage and parking facilities.

Sheraton Brussels Hotel & Towers ▯▯▯
3 place Rogier
1210 Brussels
Tel. 224 3111
Fax 224 3456
528 rooms. A luxury hotel with a roof-top swimming pool and excellent views over Brussels. Facilities include a restaurant, music bar, fitness centre, sauna, disabled access and parking.

Siru ▯-▯▯
1 place Rogier
1210 Brussels
Tel. 217 7580
Fax 218 3303
101 rooms. Decorated by 130 Belgian artists (including Marien and Somville), this hotel has a unique ambience. Each room is dedicated to the works of a particular artist. Restaurant and bar, conference facilities and parking.

The Montgomery Hotel ▯▯▯
134 avenue de Tervueren
1150 Brussels
Tel. 741 8511
Fax 741 8500
67 rooms. Luxury hotel with conference rooms, fitness centre, garage, sauna and bar.

The Stanhope Hotel ▯▯▯
9 rue du Commerce
1040 Brussels
Tel. 506 9111
Fax 512 1708
50 rooms. Quiet luxury hotel with restaurant and bar, fitness centre, sauna, garden, garage and parking.

Vendôme ▯
98 boulevard Adolphe-Max
1000 Brussels
Tel. 218 0070
Fax 218 0683
118 rooms. This is a simple but comfortable hotel with a bar, garage and parking. No restaurant.

BRUGES

Adornes ▯▯
St-Annarei 26
8000 Bruges
Tel. (050) 34 1336
Fax (050) 34 2085
20 rooms in this pleasant hotel with a tastefully decorated interior

70

and great views. Vaulted cellar. No restaurant.

Bourgoensch Hof ▯▯

Wolldestraat 39
8000 Bruges
Tel. (050) 33 1645
Fax (050) 34 6378
11 rooms. A very quiet and relaxing hotel situated in the centre. Lovely views over the canals and traditional old Flemish houses. No restaurant.

Novotel South ▯▯

Chartreuseweg 20
8200 Bruges
Tel. (050) 38 2851
Fax (050) 38 7903
111 rooms. A lovely, traditional Flemish-style building with its own garden, and overlooking the canals. Situated near the square and the métro station. Facilities include outdoor dining and swimming pool.

Orangerie ▯▯▯

Karthuizerinnestraat 10
8000 Bruges
Tel. (050) 34 1649
Fax (050) 33 3016
19 rooms. A peaceful hotel with excellent standards, set in an ancient, Flemish-style building with a well-arranged interior. Car park, breakfast room. No restaurant.

Oud Huis Amsterdam ▯▯▯

Spiegelrei 3
8000 Bruges
Tel. (050) 34 1810
Fax (050) 33 8891
22 rooms. A quiet hotel with great views over the canal. This splendid building, furnished with antique furniture, dates from around the 17th century, and was originally a Dutch trading-house. Garden, terrace and fitness centre.

Prinsenhof ▯▯

Ontvangersstraat 9
8000 Bruges
Tel. (050) 34 2690
Fax (050) 342321
16 rooms. A quiet hotel just two minutes' walk from Markt main square. Tastefully arranged interior. No restaurant.

GHENT

St Jorishof ▯▯

Botermarkt 2
9000 Ghent
Tel. (092) 224 2424
Fax (092) 24 2640
28 rooms in a renovated 18th-century building. A very attractive feature of this hotel is the restaurant, which is housed in a 13th-century Flemish-style room. Car park and terrace.

71

KNOKKE-HEIST

Les Pingouins

Duinendreef 52
8390 Knokke-Heist
Tel. (050) 51 3340
Fax (050) 51 0953
11 rooms. With its own beautiful garden, outdoor dining is a must in this hotel. A tennis court is available for the sporty. Restaurant.

Lugano

Villapad 14
8300 Knokke-Heist
Tel. (050) 61 0471
Fax (050) 62 3676
27 rooms. Quiet, tastefully decorated hotel. Lovely views, garden and outdoor dining.

Monterey

Bocheldreef 4
8390 Knokke-Heist
Tel. (050) 51 5865
Fax (050) 51 0791
9 rooms. A quiet hotel in a refurbished villa offering splendid views and a garden. No restaurant.

La Réserve

Elisabethlaan 160
8300 Knokke-Heist
Tel. (050) 61 0606
Fax (050) 60 3706
117 rooms in this recently renovated luxury hotel. Outdoor dining in the summer is available on a peaceful terrace overlooking the lake. Facilities include an indoor swimming pool, tennis court and restaurant.

Prins Boudewijn

Lippenslaan 35
8390 Knokke-Heist
Tel. (050) 60 1016
32 rooms. Conveniently situated for the station. No restaurant.

OSTEND

Andromeda

Kursaal Westhelling 5
8400 Ostend
Tel. (059) 80 6611
Fax (059) 80 6629
90 rooms. An excellent hotel built directly on the promenade and offering some outstanding views of the beach. Some of the facilities available include outdoor dining, an open-air swimming pool and restaurant.

Strand Hotel

Visserskaai I
8400 Ostend
Tel. (059) 70 3383
Fax (059) 80 3678
26 rooms in this simple, elegant and comfortable hotel with a good restaurant offering beautiful panoramic views of the sea.

Recommended Restaurants

As a general rule, many Brussels restaurants are closed from the end of July to mid-August. Do check to make certain that they are open and advance reservations are advisable. In Belgium, restaurant prices usually include service and taxes. Special features are given, as well as regular closing days.

The prices listed below refer to a 3-course meal for one consisting of a starter, a main course and a dessert and excluding service and wine. Remember that wine can increase the final bill quite considerably.

I	below BF1,100
II	BF1,100-1,700
III	above BF1,700

BRUSSELS

Amandier I
184 avenue de Fré
1180 Brussels
Tel. 374 0395
Enjoy gastronomic delights in this classic, stylish restaurant with its decor designed by Ralph Lauren. There is a separate, more informal bar upstairs. Terrace and garden. Closed Saturday lunchtime and Sunday.

Aux Armes de Bruxelles II
13 rue Bouchers
1000 Brussels
Tel. 511 5598
Quite close to Grand-Place, there is a typical Brussels atmosphere in this restaurant with its own terrace. There is an extensive menu and wine list with Brussels specialities. Open 12.00-11.15pm and closed Monday. Parking close by.

Les Baguettes Impériales II
70 avenue J. Sobieski
1020 Brussels
Tel. 479 6732
Very good quality Vietnamese cuisine in an exotic setting. Closed Sunday evening and Tuesday.

La Belle Maraîchère II
11 place Ste-Catherine
1000 Brussels
Tel. 512 9759
This restaurant is justly proud of the high standard of its cuisine, **73**

and offers seafood as its speciality. Closed Wednesday and Thursday.

Bernard IIII
93 rue Namur
1000 Brussels
Tel. 512 8821
Seafood specialities. Closed Sunday all day, Monday evening and public holidays.

Bruneau IIII
73 avenue Broustin
1080 Brussels
Tel. 427 6978
An elegant restaurant with superb nouvelle cuisine served either in a luxurious private dining room or on the terrace. Reservation is essential. Disabled access. Closed Saturday lunchtime and Monday.

Au Cheval Marin II
25 Marché-aux-Porcs
1000 Brussels
Tel. 513 0287
Seafood specialities are served in in this atmospheric establishment which is enhanced by its period decor. Closed Sunday.

Le Citron Vert I
242 avenue H. Conscience
1140 Brussels
Tel. 241 1257
Belgian specialities and salmon are served here. Reservation is essential. Some disabled facilities available. Closed Monday evening and Tuesday.

Claude Dupont IIII
46 avenue Vital-Riethuisen
1080 Brussels
Tel. 426 0000
This small yet classically elegant restaurant is run by the award-winning Claude Dupont. Excellent light cuisine and a traditional Belgian menu are served here, all attractively presented. Reservation essential. Car park. Closed Monday and Tuesday.

Comme Chez Soi IIII
23 place Rouppe
1000 Brussels
Tel. 512 2921
Superb cuisine and very popular. The luxury art nouveau interior and the Belle Epoque atmosphere, as created by the Belgian architect Horta, make this a very special place to dine. Reservation essential. Closed Sunday and Monday and from Christmas to New Year.

L'Ecailler du Palais Royal IIII
18 rue Bodenbroek
1000 Brussels
Tel. 512 8751
Excellent seafood is served at this traditional Belgian restaurant with

oyster as its main speciality. No red meat served here. Booking essential. Private parking available. Closed Sunday, most public holidays and August.

François   ‖

2 quai aux Briques
1000 Brussels
Tel. 511 6089
Notably good cuisine with superb seafood offered as the speciality. Closed Monday.

Gesuino   ‖‖‖

3 rue Fiennes
1070 Brussels
Tel. 521 5163
Elegant restaurant with wide a range of traditional Italian specialities. Closed Saturday and Sunday.

La Grignotière   ‖‖

2041 chaussée de Wavre
1160 Brussels
Tel. 672 8185
Sumptuous art deco interior and excellent cuisine. Reservation essential. Parking facilities available. Closed Sunday and Monday.

Henri Ier   ‖

181 avenue de Messidor
1180 Brussels
Tel. 345 2629
This simple old inn with grill and outdoor dining is popular for its traditional, wholesome food. Very good value. Closed Monday.

De Hoef 1627   ‖

218 rue Edith-Cavell
1180 Brussels
Tel. 374 3417
A charming seventeenth-century rustic inn with outdoor dining on the terrace and grill. Garden. Reservation is recommended. Closed Wednesday.

Jules Verne   ‖

6 Charles Hanssens
1000 Brussels
Tel. 511 1286
People come here for the friendly service as much as they do for the excellent fresh food and the varied wine list. It's no surprise that the speciality of this restaurant/brasserie with a nautical theme is fresh fish. Definitely value for money. Closed Saturday lunchtime and all day Sunday.

't Kelderke   ‖

15 Grand-Place
1000 Brussels
Tel. 513 7344
Typical Brussels/Belgian specialities and atmosphere in this 16th-century cellar establishment in the bustling centre of the Grand-Place. Open until 2am, with a jazz band daily from 10pm.

75

Chez Léon ▌

*20 boulevard du Centenaire
(Bruparck)
1020 Brussels
Tel. 478 7267*

A second Chez Léon restaurant but on a smaller scale. Brasserie decor and friendly astmosphere.

Chez Léon de Bruxelles ▌

*18 rue Bouchers
1000 Brussels
Tel. 511 1415*

Typical Brussels atmosphere with brasserie decor and terrace. Mussels are a speciality when in season. Open until midnight.

Le Marmiton ▌

*43 rue des Bouchers
1000 Brussels
Tel. 502 1864*

Rustic-style atmosphere and good, wholesome food. Open all day until 11.20pm.

La Maison du Cygne ▐▐▐

*2 rue Charles Buls
1000 Brussels
Tel. 511 8244*

Housed in a beautiful old building with a luxurious and elegant interior, and situated in Grand-Place. The service and traditional French cuisine are excellent, but expensive – save your visits for special occasions only. Closed Saturday lunchtime and Sunday.

Mon Manège à Toi ▐▐▐

*1 rue Neerveld
1200 Brussels
Tel. 770 0238*

Modern interior and excellent cuisine. Disabled access and parking facilities. Closed Saturday, Sunday and public holidays.

Quincaillerie ▌

*45 rue du Page
1050 Brussels
Tel. 538 2553*

Set in a renovated warehouse, replete with beautiful staircases and galleries, this eccentric and stylish restaurant usually attracts an 'arty' clientele.

La Salade Folle ▐▐

*9 avenue Jules Dujardin
1150 Brussels
Tel. 770 1961*

Buffet, grill and outdoor dining are the main speciality. Closed Sunday evening and Monday.

Le Sermon ▐▐

*91 avenue Jacques-Sermon
1090 Brussels
Tel. 426 8935*

Particularly good classic French cuisine served in elegant surroundings. Situated close to the centre of town. Parking facilities. Closed Sunday and Monday.

Sirène d'Or   ▯▯▯

1a place Ste-Catherine
1000 Brussels
Tel. 513 5198
A great variety of seafood is served in this excellent contemporary-style restaurant. Closed Sunday and Monday.

Trente rue de la   ▯▯▯
Paille

30 rue Paille
1000 Brussels
Tel. 512 0715
Notably good cuisine in this charming restaurant. Closed Saturday and Sunday.

La Truite d'Argent   ▯▯

23 quai au Bois à Brûler
1000 Brussels
Tel. 219 9546
Luxurious surroundings and superb food. Closed Saturday noon, Sunday and public holidays. Parking and attendant.

De Ultieme   ▯▯
Hallucinatie

Koningstraat 316 (Rue Royale)
1210 Brussels
Tel. 217 0614
An unprepossessing façade conceals a lively café popular with students and an up-market restaurant with Art Nouveau decor.

Villa d'Este   ▯▯▯

142 rue Etoile
1180 Brussels
Tel. 376 4848
Fine French classic cuisine served in a rustic-style interior. Closed Sunday evening and Monday.

Villa Lorraine   ▯▯▯

75 avenue du Vivier d'Oie
Brussels
Tel. 374 3163
Elegant classic restaurant only a short drive from the city centre and in a charming woodland setting. Excellent cuisine. Reservation is advisable. Closed Sunday.

ANTWERP

't Fornuis   ▯▯▯

Reyndersstraat 24
2000 Antwerp
Tel. (03) 233 6270
Excellent cuisine is served in this cosy, country-style establishment. Closed Saturday and Sunday.

Koperen Kete   ▯▯

Wiegstraat 5
2000 Antwerp
Tel. (03) 233 1274
French/Flemish traditional cuisine, with asparagus and lamb as **77**

the speciality in summer and game in winter. Situated in the old centre near the Cathedral. Closed on Sunday and public holidays.

Manoir

Everdijstraat 13
2000 Antwerp
Tel. (03) 232 7697
Unusual décor. Fish and lamb specialities. Closed Wednesday.

Panaché

Statiestraat 17
2018 Antwerp
Tel. (03) 232 6905
Snack bar serving hot and cold food, sandwiches, omellettes and a variety of quick meals. Open until 1.30am with seating facilities for around 100 diners.

La Pérouse

Steenplein
2000 Antwerp
Tel. (03) 231 3151
Excellent restaurant in a moored boat with beautiful views. Reservation is essential. Closed Sunday, Monday and public holidays.

Rooden-Hoed

Oude Koornmarkt 25
2000 Antwerp
Tel. (03) 233 2844
Typical Antwerp atmosphere with tasty mussels (in season) a special-

ity. Closed Wednesday and Thursday, and mid-June to mid-July.

Sir Anthony Van Dijck

Oude Koornmarkt 16
2000 Antwerp
Tel. (03) 231 6170
A tastefully furnished restaurant situated in a narrow, 16th-century alley-way. Closed all day Saturday and Sunday.

Vateli

Van Putlei 31
2018 Antwerp
Tel. (03) 238 2588
Classic restaurant serving good, wholesome food. Closed Sunday and Monday.

BRUGES

De Karmeliet

Langestraat 19
8000 Bruges
Tel. (050) 33 8259
Excellent light French cuisine in a beautiful 19th-century building. Closed Sunday evening, and Sunday lunchtime in July and August. Outdoor dining in the garden.

Weinebrugge

Koning Albertlaan 242
8200 Bruges
Tel. (050) 38 4440

Excellent French cuisine is served in the setting of a modern manor house with elegant decor. Closed Wednesday and Thursday. Advance bookings are recommended, particularly for weekends.

De Witte Poorte

Jan Van Eyckplein 6
8000 Bruges
Tel. (050) 33 0883
Traditional Belgian and French cuisine served in a 14th-century vaulted former warehouse. Closed Sunday, Monday, and one week in January and July.

De Zilveren Pauw

Zilverstraat 41
8000 Bruges
Tel. (050) 33 5566
Outdoor dining on the patio or elegant meals in the Belle Epoque interior. Closed Tuesday evening and Wednesday.

ESSENE-AFFLIGEM

Hostellerie Bellemolen

Exit 19A on E-40
1790 Essene-Affligem
Tel. (053) 66 6238
Twelfth-century mill serving especially good cuisine. Tastefully furnished. Closed Sunday evening and Monday.

GHENT

Apicius

Maurice Maeterlinckstraat 8
9000 Ghent
Tel. (092) 22 4600
Excellent cuisine in pleasant surroundings. Closed Saturday lunchtime and Sunday.

Karel De Stoute

Vrouwebroersstraat 5
900 Ghent
Tel. (092) 224 1735
Outdoor dining. Closed Saturday lunchtime and Sunday.

Ter Toren

Sint Bernadettestraat 626
900 Ghent
Tel. (092) 251 1129
Outdoor dining in a shady park. Closed Sunday evening, all day Monday and Wednesday evening.

KNOKKE-HEIST

Gasthof Katelijne

Kustlaan 166
8300 Knokke-Heist
Tel. (050) 60 1216
An old, rustic country-style inn where you can enjoy the beautiful views from the terrace along with your meal of good wholesome food. Outdoor dining is a must in good weather.

79

Hippocampus

Kragendijk 188
8300 Knokke-Heist
Tel. (050) 60 4570
An opportunity to dine in the setting of a traditional Flemish homestead with charming views. Closed Wednesday.

Petit Bedon

Zeedijk 672
3800 Knokke-Heist
Tel. (050) 60 0664
Outdoor dining and grill. Good value for money. Closed on Wednesday.

OSTEND

Lusitania

Visserskaai 35
8400 Ostend
Tel. (059) 70 1765
A rustic-style restaurant serving traditional fish and meat recipes. Be sure to have a look at the lovely collection of paintings on display here.

OVERIJSE

Barbizon

Welriekendedreef 95
3900 Overijse, Jezus-Eik
Tel. 657 0462
Outdoor dining on the terrace and good cuisine make this a most enjoyable restaurant. Garden. Reservation is essential. Closed Tuesday and Wednesday.

WATERLOO

Maison du Seigneur

389 chaussée de Tervuren
1410 Waterloo
Tel. (02) 354 0750
Dine in this picturesque Brabant-style, 17th-century farmhouse, or enjoy outdoor dining on the terrace. Parking facilities available. Closed Monday and Tuesday.

Sphinx

178 chaussée de Tervuren
1410 Waterloo
Tel. (02) 354 1969
Enjoy French cuisine indoors or on the terrace. Parking and disabled facilities. Closed Tuesday evening and Wednesday.

WEMMEL

Eddie Van Maele

964 chaussée Romaine
1810 Wemmel
Tel. 460 6145
The flower-filled terrace and garden of this quaint yet elegant restaurant make dining a pleasant experience. Reservation essential. Closed Saturday lunchtime, Sunday and Monday.

By the 12th century, Ghent had developed into the largest textile centre in the world and become a wealthy town. Several centuries later, the residents could not accept the high taxes Charles V tried to impose on them without a fight. Indeed, history shows that the people of Ghent have never enjoyed being taken for granted. Once they had made their fortune in the wool trade, they sided with their suppliers, the English, against the French. An ambitious restoration programme currently sustains the Gothic and Renaissance splendours of Ghent's past, while promoting modern industrial and urban expansion.

When you reach the town, head straight for the middle of the **Sint-Michielsbrug** (St Michael's Bridge). From this perfect vantage point you can look around 360 degrees over one of the most delightful urban vistas in the world. To the east can be seen the three towers of St Bavon's Cathedral, and the belfry and Church of

---

The Itinerant Lamb

The van Eyck masterpiece has not had an easy life. The people of Ghent had to protect it from the thieving hands of Philip II and the iconoclastic flames of the Protestants. Emperor Joseph II, who prided himself on being an enlightened liberal, was embarrassed by the nudity of Adam and Eve on the painting's side-panels, so the panels were removed. The French revolutionaries carried the painting off to Paris and it took Waterloo to get it back. The Church then sold the side-panels, which ended up in Germany in the private collection of the king of Prussia, and were later given to a Berlin museum. The Treaty of Versailles returned the painting to the Belgian state, and by 1920 the complete work could be admired. It disappeared again after German occupation of Belgium but was found, side-panels and all, in some Tyrolean salt mines and returned to Ghent, with Adam and Eve once again blissfully naked.

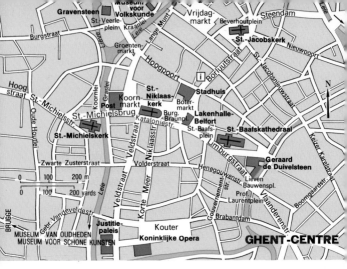

St Nicholas; to the south, the apse of the Church of St Michael and its reflection in the River Lieve; to the north the ominous crenellated ramparts and turrets of the Gravensteen, castle of the counts of Flanders; and immediately below you, the weathered façades of the old Flemish-Gothic and Renaissance merchants' houses of the Graslei (Grass Quay) on the right and the Koornlei (Corn Quay) on the left.

The architectural glory of Ghent, on a very human scale, is the **Graslei**, whose houses are a marvel of subtle colour,

graceful form and ornamental detail. As you look from the bridge, from right to left, you can see the **House of the Free Bargemen**. Its gently curving roof dating from 1531, modifies the traditional right-angled crow-steps of Flemish-Gothic, giving an almost baroque flavour to the upper storey. Right next to that you will see the large, red-brick **House of the Grain Measurers** (1698), and the smaller **Toll-House**, where a fee in grain was paid for right of passage on the river, and then, in complete contrast to the surrounding buildings, the oldest, an austere Romanesque **Warehouse** of 1200. Of the houses on the other bank, the **Koornlei**, the most appealing is the **House of the 'Unfree' Bargemen** (who did not enjoy the privileges of Free Bargemen) at No. 7, a late-baroque house of 1740.

Take a walk back from St Michael's Bridge to the imposing 15th-century **Lakenhalle** (Drapers' Hall), centre of Ghent's ancient prosperity. In the huge Gothic assembly hall, you can see a multilingual 'sound-and-light' show called 'Ghent and Charles V'. It recounts the story of the city's steadfast refusal to pay taxes to finance the wars of the emperor, despite the fact that he was born in Ghent.

Soaring above the Lakenhalle is the great 90m (300ft) **Belfort** (belfry), symbol since 1321 of the town's civic freedoms and a visual challenge to the cathedral, whose spiritual power was more often allied with that of the reigning monarch, duke or emperor.

The **Stadhuis** (Town Hall) is a strange but not unattractive combination of the late-Gothic Charter House facing on to Hoogpoort and a Renaissance wing facing Botermarkt to the east. The Gothic façade is as decorative as a flamboyant cathedral, with a splendid balcony for proclamations, while the Renaissance façade is far more stately, almost solemn, with elegant lattice windows flanking the staircase to its high-columned doorway.

Sint-Baafskathedraal (St Bavon's Cathedral) is without doubt one of the finest Gothic churches of the Low Countries, a harmonious and subtly-hued structure of buttermilk and grey stone and red brick. Construction began in the 13th century (the choir) and was completed in the 16th century with the tower (which unfortunately lost its steeple in a fire in 1603).

The artistic jewel of its interior is **The Adoration of the Mystic Lamb** (1432), a huge altar painting by Jan van Eyck (with possible additions by his brother Hubert) in the baptistery. This monumental work celebrates a wonderful church **83** with some superb portraits of the donors, saints, princes and prophets of the church all surrounding the hallowed Lamb, symbol of redemption, above the fountain of life. The landscape is a botanists' delight, depicting around 42 different plants, while the 'Jerusalem' of the background has been identified as a composite skyline of Utrecht, Bruges, Mainz and Cologne.

Ghent is home to two intriguing old castles. **Geraard de Duivelsteen** (Castle of Gerard the Devil) overlooks the River Schelde on Bauwens square. This forbidding 13th-century construction, known in its time for the nasty torture chambers, now houses the old, dusty state archives of western Flanders. The **Gravensteen**, the moated castle of the counts of Flanders, is perhaps more varied in its design, which took place between the 9th and

12th centuries, but it can boast just as unpleasant a history as Gerard's place. Take a look, if you dare, at the dungeons and the gruesome museum of instruments of torture, with head shrinkers (in iron), leg-irons, straitjackets, ball and chains and ankle braces. There is a splendid view from the terrace at the top, from which they often launched cannonballs

A tour by river boat is one of the most relaxing ways to see the old town of Ghent.

and poured boiling oil over enemies through the centuries.

In the same vein, you can also admire the **Dulle Griet** (Angry Maggie), an enormous 13-tonne iron cannon, displayed near the Vrijdagmarkt (Friday market). During the 15th century this huge monster was used to fire stone balls weighing around 320kg (750lbs). Its destructive power might well have inspired Brueghel's violent painting of the war of the same name, now on view in the Mayer van den Bergh Museum in Antwerp (see p.63).

To restore your peace of mind a little, why not visit one of the many colourful **markets** Ghent has to offer almost every day of the week all over town – a great variety of fruits and vegetables, flowers, birds,

domestic pets and poultry, cattle and a lively flea market on the Beverhout square just beside St-Jacobskerk, the city's oldest church.

Of Ghent's many **museums**, the following are the most interesting. The Museum voor Volkskunde (Folklore) housed in a 14th-century children's home, Kraanlei 63, offers an intimate glimpse of the past, along with a fascinating series

of 19th-century traditional Flemish interiors.

The most outstanding works on display at the Museum voor Schone Kunsten (Fine Arts), on De Liemaeckereplein 3, are two magnificent paintings by Hieronymus Bosch – *Saint Jerome* and *The Bearing of the Cross*, in which Jesus is almost lost amid the ugly, menacing crowd surrounding him. There is also an excellent tapestry room displaying a variety of works from Brussels' golden era of the 17th century.

Arguably the best museum in Ghent, Museum van Oudheden (Godshuizenlaan 2), is housed in the exquisite medieval Abbey of Bijloke and contains an intriguing collection of artefacts. Make sure you take the time to visit the beautiful gabled refectory and wander around the restored Renaissance garden, leaving Angry Maggie far behind you.

This sinister medieval castle was once famous for its gruesome torture chambers.

BRUGES

Population 137,000

Bruges (*Brugge* in Flemish) is, quite simply, the prettiest town in Belgium and one of the prettiest in Europe. It's a town to walk in, to take a boat ride in, and to do everything in a leisurely fashion. It's a town where civilization takes on a more dignified meaning.

When you wander around Bruges, past the charming, old houses and along the banks of the canals, stand on the bridge over the Minnewater and look back at the Begijnhof, the cathedral and further beyond to the belfry and the Town Hall,

all so solid, peaceful and immovable, you may ask yourself, why can't the whole world be like this?

This air of blessed apartness did not come easily. Things began well enough, with the Zwin inlet making Bruges a desirable protected port for international trade during the Middle Ages and certainly attractive enough for the king of France, Philip the Fair, to grab it from the count of Flanders in 1297. In fact, when Philip arrived in town, the ladies of Bruges turned out so elegantly to receive him that his wife threw a jealous tantrum. However the men of Bruges didn't

The Swan Song Goes On

In 1488 the people of Bruges rebelled against Archduke Maximilian of Austria, throwing him in prison and chopping off the head of his counsellor, Pieter Lanchals. To avoid a similar fate, Maximilian promised to satisfy the citizens' complaints and was released. He immediately ordered that the people of Bruges keep in perpetuity a flock of swans in expiation of Lanchals' death (his name meant 'long neck' and his coat of arms bore a swan). Unlike Maximilian, the people kept their side of the bargain, and today the swans still parade with a B for Bruges and their date of birth marked on their beaks.

87

want any part of the French. Their angry revolt against the invaders in May 1302 took the form of a tongue-twister. Anyone who couldn't pronounce the war cry *'Schild en vriend'* (shield and friend) with the right guttural turns had to be a Frenchman, and was therefore slaughtered.

Bruges came into its own as a port, a transit point for the great Hanseatic League, shipping coal, wool and cheese from England, wine from Germany, furs from Russia, metal from Poland and the Balkans, and spices from the Orient. However, the prosperity only lasted until the end of the 15th century, when the Zwin silted up. Consequently, the Flemish cloth industry collapsed, trade routes changed and Bruges was eclipsed by Antwerp. It slumbered until the end of the 19th century, admired only by lugubrious Romantic writers who loved the melancholy decadence of 'Bruges-la-Morte'.

The building of the port of Zeebrugge in 1907, linked by canal to Bruges, brought about a spectacular revival.

The picturesque old town of Bruges has been a haven for artists since the 15th century.

If you're coming to Bruges by car, you best bet is to park at your hotel, or at the station (no charge, 10 minutes' walk from the centre). Alternatively, there are a number of car parks where you will have to pay a fee. Do not try to park at the Markt. There are just two ways to see the town – on foot and in a boat – and you should really try both. Boats leave from four embarcation points, the Vismarkt, Rozenhoedkaai, the Dyver and the Gruuthusebrug, all located south and south west of the Town Hall. Try the half-hour boat trips, which run all day long, as the perfect introduction to this lovely town.

When you're ready to walk, start at the **Markt**, the main square or *grand-place,* which is so characteristic of Belgian cities. In the centre is a 19th-century monument to Pieter de Coninck and Jan Breydel, who

led the revolt against the French in 1302. They were defending the hard-earned privileges of the corporations and the trade profits, symbolized by the magnificent weathered brick **Halle** (covered market) and **Belfort** (belfry) which dominate the square today.

The 13th-century Halle and belfry have survived in shining splendour despite the town's ups and downs. Above the entrance to the belfry is a large balcony from which the magistrates read their proclamations before the people summoned by the great bells. You can see these if you climb the 80m (402 steps) to the top. Concerts are held here in summer (Monday, Wednesday, Saturday 9pm; Sunday 2.15pm).

Opposite the Halle, on the north side of the square, are some fine corporation houses from the 17th century, the best perhaps being the House of the Fishmongers, with anchors decorating its gabled façade. **39**

The **Stadhuis** (Town Hall) of Bruges, begun in 1376, set the architectural pattern for all Flanders' citadels of municipal power – its main square is still known as 'Burg' or 'fortress'.

The grand building thrusts inexorably upwards with elegant turrets, tall, narrow windows bearing the coats of arms of surrounding towns subject to Bruges' domination during the Middle Ages, and the slim, erect statuary of historic heroes. Every single line in the structure proclaims the town's imperturbable civic pride. Indeed, there is a balcony on the right where the counts of Flanders came to take their oath of fidelity to the town's inalienable civic liberties.

Inside, on the ground floor, you will see several sculptures of the biblical prophets and get the feeling that the town's aldermen must have identified strongly with these formidable forefathers. To remove every doubt, take a look at the 14th-century **Gothic Room** on the first floor with its magnificent vaulted wooden ceiling. The place still brims with dignity.

To the left of the town hall is the former palace of the Free Council of Bruges, previously home to the law courts and now housing the tourist office. Although transformed in the 18th century, a splendid 16th-century façade overlooking the canal remains. You should also visit the Council Chamber for its fine Renaissance fireplace of black marble, oak and white alabaster. It was built to celebrate Charles V's victory of 1525 over François I at Pavia. Charles himself has pride of place among the sculptures, brandishing his sword amidst life-size statues of his ancestors, Ferdinand and Isabella of Spain to the left, and Maximilian of Austria and Marie of Burgundy to the right. A lovely alabaster frieze of the biblical story of Susannah and the old men adorns the mantlepiece, and just below are three ornately carved copper rings which the aldermen held on to while dangling their muddy boots to dry off near the fire.

Your best view of the façade is from the Steenhouwersdijk next to the still-operative Vismarkt (fish market). To the east is the lovely **Groene Rei** (Green Canal) with its border of tree-lined gardens and its rickety-looking hump-backed bridges, which are in reality very sturdy. This is a charming place to sit and savour. Look back to the great towers of the St-Salvator cathedral, of Onze Lieve Vrouwekerk (church of Notre-Dame) and of the belfry, and then just relax among the quaint little dwellings for the elderly, **De Pelikaan** (1714), named after the bird you will find in a bas-relief over the main entrance.

Walk back to the **Rozenhoedkaai** (Rosary Quay), and pause for a while on the bridge (Sint-Jan Nepomucenusbrug) commemorating the throwing of the Archbishop of Prague into the River Moldau. From the bridge continue on to the **Dyver**, with each stretch of tree-shaded canal bank offer-

ing a new and gently changing perspective of intimate gabled houses, ivy-covered bridges and that public, civic, ecclesiastical skyline behind to remind you of the outside world.

The Dyver takes you to the **Groeninge Museum,** which houses a superb collection of early Flemish painting, mostly from the 15th-century Primitive School of which Bruges was a celebrated centre. **Jan**

A delightful view over the steeply sloping roofs and stepped gables of old Bruges.

*M*emling's painting of the Madonna and Child, from the Memling Museum in Bruges.

van Eyck is represented by two of his master works, *The Madonna and The Canon van der Paele*, painted in 1436, and *Margareta van Eyck* (1439), a marvellously frank, unidealized portrait of his wife. Other important paintings include a moving *Death of the Virgin* **92** by **Hugo van der Goes**; *The Annunciation* in two separate panels depicting Gabriel and Mary, by **Hans Memling**, as well as his great Moreel triptych showing St Christopher carrying Jesus, with side panels of the prolific Burgomaster Moreel and his wife with their five sons and eleven daughters; a *Baptism of Christ* triptych by Gerard David; and the poignant *The Last Judgment* by Hieronymus Bosch. The entire career of Jan van Eyck, who spent most of his adult life in Bruges, is depicted in an excellent slide presentation.

Next to the museum is the fine old Gruuthuse (House of Groats – the fermented barley used in the brewing of beer), now a small museum of arts and crafts. The walk continues through to the church of **Onze Lieve Vrouw**, a little austere in the framework of Bruges' architecture, but worthy of attention for an early sculpture of Michelangelo, *The Virgin and the Child*, in the chapel of the Virgin. The Lanchals Chapel contains the tombs of Charles the Bold and Marie of Burgundy. Her sudden death in a riding accident in 1482 at the age of 25 left the Low Countries in the hands of the Habsburgs. Look out also for two fine paintings by the 15th-century Cologne master Stefan Lochner, *The Adoration of the Magi* and *The Annunciation*.

The **St-Salvator** cathedral suffered four great fires in the 800 years of its history, as well as the ravages of the Calvinists, so that very little of its old glory remains. The choir, however, has managed to retain some of its beautifully carved 15th-century stalls, fine Brussels' tapestries and Bishop Carondelet's 16th-century tombstone. The cathedral's museum holds two noteworthy pieces by the artists Hugo van der Goes and Dirk Bouts.

Bruges is almost as proud of Hans Memling, who moved here in 1477, as Antwerp is of Rubens. A **Memling Museum** is installed in the old St-Jans-hospitaal (hospital of St John), where the artist was cared for after being badly injured at the Battle of Nancy. While recovering from his wounds, Memling painted the *Reliquary of St Ursula* in secret and gave it to the hospital in gratitude for his recovery. These six paintings on a sculpted wood casket in the form of a Gothic chapel are now the centre-piece of the museum, and tell how Ursula and 11,000 virgins travelled to Rome and were massacred by the pagans of Cologne on their way back. Another highlight is Memling's magnificent altarpiece, *Mystical Marriage of St Catherine*, with side panels devoted to St John the Evangelist and St John the Baptist, the hospital's patrons.

93

Walk down the lively shopping street, Katelijnestraat, until the Wijngaardstraat turns to the right onto a little square. Cross the hump-backed bridge to the 18th-century gateway of the **Begijnhof**, a nunnery founded in 1245 by Margaret of Constantinople. Suddenly you're in yet another of those places where you feel far away from it all – though after a while in Bruges you begin to forget what it is you left behind. For centuries this blessed haven of peace housed the Beguines, pious women who devoted their lives to prayer and such delicate industry as lacemaking or weaving. In 1930, the last of the Beguines died and Benedictine nuns took

The tradition of labour and meditation in the Begijnhof has continued unbroken since 1245.

their place, but continued the tradition of tranquil labour and meditation. These days you can walk among the trees – and daffodils in springtime – and visit one of the little white houses of the cloister, with its spartanly furnished bedroom, living-room decorated with religious paintings, and kitchen overlooking a small garden.

If your own meditation tends more to the gently profane than to the sacred, your visit to Bruges will end blissfully at the **Minnewater** (Lake of Love) just south of the Begijnhof. If the latter is blessed, the Minnewater is most definitely charmed by the most benign of pagan spirits, a cool expanse of still water, the perfect place for quiet walks, for whispered poems, and for lying on the grass and staring up through the trees at nothing in particular as the swans glide silently by.

At the southern end of the Minnewater is a bridge where the Ghent Canal begins. Next to the bridge is a 15th-century gunpowder house for the defence of the old ramparts.

The Coast

If you've been walking around a lot, you'll be ready for a rest on the beach. Belgium's coast on the North Sea is as bracing as any in Europe. Because of the iodine in the salty air, they say that the suntan you get on the beaches between Ostend and Knokke-Heist lasts longer than the more expensive brand from the Côte d'Azur.

Ostend (Oostende/Ostende) is a jolly seaside town with a whiff of the naughty nineties and the Belle Epoque along its Albert I Promenade, from the Kursaal (Casino) to the Hippodrome, a whiff that mixes pungently with oysters, cockles, mussels and suntan lotion. The beaches have some charming old-fashioned sunbathing huts, parasols and deckchairs lined up in colourful rows that look, from the promenade, like battalions of toy soldiers.

Boat lovers will enjoy wandering around the **port**, and can visit the Belgian merchant navy's port training ship. The fishing fleet unloads its catch early in the morning at the **95**

Not quite the Med – but with a deck-chair and windbreak, you will enjoy the beach.

minque (fish market), where around 50 million kg (110 million lbs) of fish are sold each year. The sole are particularly good and well worth a try.

If you haven't yet had your fill of culture, then visit the fine arts museum at the **Feestpaleis** for a look at the weird and wonderful work of Ostend's own James Ensor. This extensive collection is made up of around 20 paintings, 80 drawings and over 100 etchings of vibrant satire, and successfully captures that special Belgian mixture of the grim and the hilarious. **Ensorhuis** (Ensor's home) at Vlaanderenstraat 27 has been converted into a museum recreating his studio on the top floor.

If you are in need of a quiet swim, move on to **Bredene**, where you will find the most beautiful sand dunes, ideal for camping, fishing or just relaxing. On the way, you can visit the cruiser the *Vindictive*, that came to grief defending Ostend in 1918. People looking for family hotels usually go on to **Blankenberge**, with all the fun of the fair at the Luna Park. On rainy days, there's always the aquarium.

The chic spot on the coast is **Knokke-Heist** – with elegant shops, luxurious hotels, and expensive nightclubs. The casino, it seems, has the world's

biggest chandelier, made of Venetian crystal with around 2,000 lights. Further east, in the exclusive district known as the Zoute, you will see some dazzling resort villas, their immaculate lawns protected by stringent legislation in order to keep out property developers.

Between Knokke and the Dutch border is the delightful nature reserve of the **Zwin**, a long stretch of about 145ha (360 acres) of sand dunes and grassland reclaimed from the sea when Bruges lost its inland waterway. Open to the public, the Zwin shelters around 300 species of bird, including rare storks, herons and geese saved from the threat of extinction by the resident ornithologists. The birds can best be observed during springtime, the countless varieties of flowers and plants in the summer, and any time of the year you will see hundreds of wild rabbits. **97**

What to Do

Shopping

In these days of standardization, it is difficult to pinpoint what distinctive presents you can buy in Brussels and won't find anywhere else. However, there are still a few specialities to look out for.

Although inflation has sent costs sky-high and Brussels' own international community has pushed the prices up even higher, it is Belgium's home-grown products that offer the most attractive prices. You will discover that this is true both in the elegant boutiques of Avenue Louise and the Galeries St-Hubert and in the more popular shops of Les Marolles and the large department stores on Boulevard Adolphe Max and Rue Neuve.

In the general movement to rediscover old arts and crafts, **lace** is coming back into vogue and the best is found in Brussels and Bruges. Much of it is machine made, copies of old patterns, but you can still find hand-made work of exquisite quality, as well as innovative patterns in modern styles.

Tapestry is also machine-made these days but, if you're prepared to pay a lot, there are still some hand-made pieces to be found around the Sablon antique dealers and art galleries – expensive, but still a better buy than elsewhere.

Both **glassware** and **crystal** from Charleroi, Malines and Liège (Val St-Lambert) are on sale in the fine shops on the Avenue Louise and the other *grands boulevards*. **Pewter** is usually brought in from Huy. Quality **leather** goods are still a Brussels speciality.

If you're thinking of making an investment in either **gold** or **silver**, but in something other than ingots and coins, Brussels is of course still a great centre for jewellery and other pieces of superb craftsmanship. You might also want to pause in your sightseeing in Antwerp for a side-trip to the **diamond** market. There you'll see a fabulous selection of the world's most exorbitant trinkets.

More modest, but no less artistic, is the finely wrought **ironware** from Brussels and Antwerp, where excellent reproductions of medieval fire-screens are made.

Wooden toys are a flourishing craft in Spa, Verviers, and can be bought in Brussels.

All these products are, of course, available brand new, but **antique** originals can also be seen in the experts' shops on the Sablon and at the flea markets – in Les Marolles on the Place du Jeu de Balle (every morning except Mondays), in Antwerp at St Jacob's Church, and in Ghent on the Beverhoutsplein. You needn't be afraid to bargain – it's expected of you.

Belgium offers a tempting array of **edible souvenirs**. The most famous are the custom-made *pralines*, luscious filled

Belgian chocolates – the most popular but also the most short-lived of souvenirs.

*P*orcelain replicas of traditional Flemish buildings always make a good present.

Place, and the markets for absolutely everything in Ghent, from chickens to flowers to cattle (see p.85).

chocolates. From the coast comes a hard sweet known as *babeluttes*. You'll also find a variety of typical Belgian biscuits – almond, honey and spice (*speculoos*).

The **markets** are a real delight wherever you go – try and visit the bird and flower markets on Brussels' Grand-

Sports

Belgium is not ashamed of its description as '*le plat pays*' (the flat country). This topographical feature has given rise to a national sport – and one that many visitors can very happily take to – **cycling**. Even if you are not up to Tour de France standard yet, you can easily buy yourself a little cap, strap a bag onto your back and take off on your own personal road race.

Bicycles are available for rental at the railway station in almost every town, especially at the seaside where it's the preferred means of transport. In Ostend, they seem to favour tricycles for two. One of the best rides is from Knokke-Heist along the sea wall to the Dutch border and back.

If cycling is too slow for you, another great sport on the Belgian coast is **sand-sailing**.

With a good wind blowing in from the North Sea, you can whip along the beach at the most fantastic speeds.

Watersports are popular, from the sedate pedalo to the more adventurous windsurfing and water-skiing, the latter not just at the seaside but also on the River Schelde at Antwerp and on the River Meuse. It is easy to rent boats for sailing at Zeebrugge or at Blankenberge and Ostend. If you would like a rowboat, then try the lakes in the Brussels parks of Bois de la Cambre, Woluwe and Tervuren, or the Lac de Genval in the Forêt de Soignes.

To go **fishing** inland, you'll need a permit (easily obtained from the post office). On the coast you can usually wangle your way onto a fishing boat at Ostend or Zeebrugge for deep-sea fishing. The rivers and canals are very well stocked with fish ranging from trout, carp, pike, chubb and roach.

The Forest of Soignes is the perfect place for **horse riding**. The Brussels Tourist Office will provide you with detailed information about where to hire a horse for the day and also about the organized 'Belgium on Horseback' tours that last from 2 to 12 days.

Hikers can follow a network of marked trails across the countryside. For further details contact the Comité National Belge des Sentiers de Grande Randonnée (B.P. 10, 4000 Liège).

Golf courses can be be found at Tervuren, in Ghent at Sint-Martens-Latem, in Antwerp at Kapellenbos, in Ostend at Klemskerke, and also in Knokke-Heist.

Public **tennis** facilities are available and the tourist office or your hotel should be able to help you find a court. You will probably find whites are *de rigueur*.

The major spectator sports are **soccer**, with a world-class team at Anderlecht; **motor racing** with the Grand Prix at Francorchamps, near Spa; and **horse-racing**, which you can usually watch at Groenendael and Boitsfort, with steeplechase at Waregem. At Ostend the racing is held at the Hippodrome Wellington.

Entertainment

Music plays an important part in Brussels' cultural life and **opera** is of a high international standard at the historic Théâtre de la Monnaie. Reversing the more usual trend of Belgian artists seeking fame in France, the great Marseilles choreographer Maurice Béjart made Brussels his home for over 20 years. His magnificent and innovative **ballet** troupe attracted fans from all over the world and created a dance tradition that is sure to continue. Orchestral **concerts** and recitals are usualy held at the Palais des Beaux-Arts and outdoors on the Grand-Place during the spring and summer.

Theatre, both classical and experimental, has more than 30 stages to choose from in the capital. Typically the Théâtre National on the Place Rogier has a repertory (in French)

*T*he Théâtre de la Monnaie is well known in Europe for the high standard of its opera productions.

which includes Harold Pinter, Samuel Beckett and Tennessee Williams as well as Molière and Maeterlinck.

A special Brussels attraction is the highly sophisticated and robustly popular **puppet theatre**, Théâtre de Toone, on an impasse off the Petite Rue des Bouchers. This tiny theatre with over 150 years of tradition, has a programme offering *Macbeth*, *Faust* and *The Count of Monte Cristo,* full of boisterous humour and gripping pathos, and delivered in an odd mixture of Brussels patois and classical French. The exquisite costumes and broad gestures make it a joy for children and adults alike.

There are countless **nightclubs** and **discothèques** scattered all over town, most of them with a surprisingly short life span. You will usually find the fashionable ones scattered around the Avenue Louise and the Chaussée de Waterloo, the more discreet ones around the Sablon and the more brassy around the Place de Brouckère. On the coast your best bet is at Knokke.

Cinemas in Brussels and elsewhere in Belgium have the added advantage of showing all films in their original version, with subtitles in French and Dutch. Kinepolis, in Bruparck (see p.106) offers one of the largest selections in Europe, some on wide screen. The Palais des Beaux-Arts has an excellent *cinémathèque* of 'collectors' items'.

Festivals

Entertainment in Belgium also means the enormously popular festivals – celebrations of folklore often derived from an obscure historical or religious event that today makes a good excuse for a procession, some extravagant fireworks, a little bit of dancing, dressing up and a party for everybody.

Brussels' own biggest festivity is the Ommegang, held around the first week in July, when the flags and banners of the corporations and the old Chambers of Rhetoric are paraded to recreate the pageant which Charles V witnessed in **103**

1549. The Grand-Place is also the site of a score of other festivities: a Begonia Festival on 15 August which covers the square in a magnificent carpet of flowers, concerts, dances and anything the city fathers manage to lay their hands on to keep the happy party going through spring and summer. For some reason they even plant the May Tree, *Meyboom*, on 9 August.

Along the coast, **Blankenberge** has a Port Festival either in May or June and a mass to bless the sea in July. On the last Sunday in August it holds a beautiful flower procession. Mardi Gras is a big occasion here, as it is throughout the whole of Belgium.

Ostend holds a big charity ball, known as the Ball of the Dead Rat, at the Casino with costumes and masks inspired by the artist, James Ensor, one of the ball's originators. On the same night the competing Shrimp Ball is held in the fishermen's district, preceded by a very grand procession. Ostend's mass for the sea is held on the last Sunday in June. Ostend also has an international festival which is held throughout July and August.

Bruges' great festivity, held on Ascension Day in May, is the *Heilig-Bloedprocessie* (the Procession of the Holy Blood), honouring a great relic said to contain drops of Christ's blood brought back from Jerusalem after the Crusades by the count of Flanders in 1150. Experts have established that the relic came from Constantinople one hundred years later, but in true Belgian spirit, the procession goes on nevertheless.

Mardi Gras in Bruges is celebrated on the preceding Saturday with a grand procession and dancing in the streets. The canals are brilliantly lit up on weekends through the month of May and then on every evening throughout the summer months. There is also a fine sound-and-light show held at the Gruuthuse from the beginning of July to mid-September.

Belgium's **national holiday** is 21 July, and there is plenty of merry-making as everybody celebrates this event in their own unique way.

CALENDAR OF EVENTS

For details on events and festivals, contact the Belgian National Tourist Office, 63 Rue du Marché-aux-Herbes (tel. 504 0390). Other sources are *BBB Agenda* and the English-language publication *The Bulletin*.

January: Antiques Fair (Palais des Beaux-Arts); Brussels International Film Festival (Palais des Congrès)

March: Brussels International Fantasy Film Festival (Auditorium 44); Ball of the Dead Rat and Shrimp Ball (Ostend); Mardi Gras celebrations (events throughout Belgium, notably in Binche)

April-May: 'Music and Light' shows (Grand-Place); Queen Elizabeth International Music Competition held every two years – odd years (Palais des Beaux-Arts); occasional public opening of the Royal Greenhouses of Laeken

May: Jazz Rallye held on last weekend of the month (events throughout Brussels); *Heilig-Bloedprocessie* (Procession of the Holy Blood) held on Ascension Day (Bruges)

May or June: Port festival (Blankenberge)

July: Ommegang first Tue and Thur of the month (Grand-Place); Belgian National Day Fireworks on 21 July (Place des Palais)

July-August: International Festival (Ostend)

July-mid-September: 'Sound and Light' show (Gruuthuse, Bruges); public access to the Royal Palace (Place des Palais) from end of June to beginning of September

August: Planting of the Meiboom (May Tree) 9 August (Brussels centre); Flower Carpet held every two years on 15 August – even years (Grand-Place); flower procession on last Sun (Blankenberge)

September: Festival of Flanders/Wallonia: classical music (events throughout Belgium); Architectural Heritage Day (events throughout Belgium)

September-December: Europalia: exhibitions and cultural events devoted to a particular country. Held every two years – odd years (events throughout Belgium)

November: Belga Jazz Festival (Brussels)

December: 'Music and Light' shows (Grand-Place); Christmas Market second weekend before Christmas (Sablon)

Children in Brussels

Brussels has two leisure parks – Bruparck and Walibi – with a range of activities to keep children entertained for the whole day, whatever the weather.

Bruparck (open April-December) is the home of **Mini-Europe**: a huge park with over 300 detailed models of famous European buildings from the Leaning Tower of Pisa to the British Houses of Parliament. Models and sound effects add to the experience: a miniature train rushes through the park and every 5 minutes the Ariane rocket blasts off in a cloud of smoke and flames. There are footpaths, rest areas and a restaurant (see p.29).

Also sited in Bruparck is **L'Océade**, a big water funpark with excellent indoor and outdoor pools, high-speed slides and wavepools, and – for the less energetic – jacuzzis, solariums and relaxing saunas. It's usually open all day during the summer, but your ticket entitles you only to a 4-hour visit (tel: 478 4320).

Look out for **The Village** in Bruparck – an area of old-style shops, taverns and restaurants together with a number of children's playgrounds. Children and adults can enjoy the ultimate cinema experience at the Imax theatre in the nearby Kinepolis complex.

Some 19km from Brussels is **Walibi** – an adventure park with about 40 rides and shows. The park also contains **Aqualibi** – a heated indoor complex with a wave-pool, jet stream and slide tunnels, as well as jacuzzis and sunbeds. During the summer Aqualibi is open every day and is reserved exclusively for visitors to Walibi (tel: 41 4466). Take the train to Bierges (Ottignies to Louvain-la-Neuve line); Walibi is 300m (330yds) from the station.

Some of the **museums**, such as Autoworld, will appeal to children. The Royal Art and History museum is home to 'Dynamuseum' (on Saturday morning and Wednesday afternoon), aimed at children from 6 to 12 years old. The Belgian Royal Institute for Natural Sciences exhibits dinosaurs and other animals, and holds workshops for children from 5 to 12 years of age. In addition, the Children's Museum, 15 rue du Bourgmestre, runs workshops on painting, collage and theatre for children (but is closed during August, tel: 640 0107).

Children will always enjoy Brussels' many **parks**. In particular, the Bois de La Cambre has a boating lake, Josaphat Park has areas for sporting activities and young people, and Mellaerts Ponds in Woluwe Park has mini-golf and boating. There are also three children's farms in the city. Ask the Tourist and Information Office for details (see p.137).

Several theatre companies stage Brussels' famous puppet shows for young and old (contact The Information Centre for Young People's Theatre, tel: 648 3458). The Théâtre Peruchet also has a puppet museum (tel: 673 8730).

The largest travelling fun-fair in Belgium sets up for the day in Les Marolles in Brussels.

Eating Out

Let's deal now with that old cliché about the Belgians eating only mussels and French fries washed down with beer. While this is far from the truth, it is worth stating that the mussels are excellent, the French fries are the best in Europe and the beer is varied enough to rival the other great beer centres of Germany and the Czech Republic.

The **mussels** (*moules*: for Flemish terms see p.113) from the North Sea are brought in fresh every day to Brussels. Served steamed in a seasoned broth, they can be a meal in themselves. The **French fries** (*frites*) are crispy and succulent, with that crackly finish insisted on by any connoisseur.

The **beer** isn't just beer: it is the national ambrosia. In a country where the average per capita consumption runs to almost 150 litres (265 pints) a year – compared with 45 litres (80 pints) in France – brewing has become as fine an art as the making of a great Bor-

108

deaux. The barley and hops that go into the malting and yeasting are picked and sorted with a refinement of technique that goes back to the monasteries which controlled a beer monopoly in the Middle Ages.

Restaurants

The Belgians' healthy appetite for the good life demands of their restaurants the very highest quality, drawing on the traditions of neighbouring French cuisine, but adding ingenious new touches derived from regional products.

The best Brussels restaurants are certainly expensive, but you will get your money's worth. The managers, cooks and waiters take pride in what they serve, whether in the simplest bistrot or the most luxurious establishment.

For light meals, there are many taverns and cafés where you can simply have a glass of beer or wine with some cold cuts of meat, sausage, pâté or cheese and a small salad.

While the more up-market restaurants have an elegance

that demands that men wear at least a jacket if not a tie and that women dress with equal formality, the atmosphere in most popular bistros is usually very relaxed. The accent is always on enjoyment.

Generally, the portions are enormous and you will usually be offered more. The trick is to take a modest amount the first time and then you can keep everybody happy by digging in heartily for the second helping. An order of pâté, for instance, comes in the form of the whole terrine with a knife and smiling instructions to help yourself. Soup bowls tend to be simply bottomless.

There have been countless attempts to explain the huge appetites of the Belgians, the most convincing being that

Belgian restaurants always guarantee a great atmosphere, fresh seafood and huge portions.

they combine the natural sturdy capacity of other northern European peoples with the stimulation of Gallic finesse in what's placed before them.

Local Specialities

Among **hors d'œuvres**, there is of course a beer soup (*soupe à la bière*) with chicken stock and onions; a kind of cold pâté of veal, pork and rabbit known as *potjesvlees*; *flamiche*, a savoury cheese pie with leeks or onions; *tomate aux crevettes*, tomato filled with shrimps and mayonnaise, and *croquettes de crevette*; and fine smoked ham (*jambon d'Ardennes*).

The best-known **main dish** is probably *waterzooi*, a chicken (or sometimes fish) stewed with whites of leeks, bouillon, cream and egg yolks. *Anguille au vert* is eel flavoured with green herbs, most popularly sorrel, sage and parsley. *Carbonnades flamandes* consists of lean beef browned in a pan and then cooked in a casserole with lots of onions and beer. *Hochepot*, a pot-au-feu based on oxtail or pigs' trotters, ears

Beer is Good for You

It all started in the 11th century with good old St Arnold. The Pope sent him back to his native Flanders to protect the people against a pillaging baron and his armies. Arnold did the job so well that the people asked him to stay and found an abbey at Oudenburg, not far from Bruges. There he noticed that the people were dying like flies from drinking the polluted water of the local river, while the beer-drinking layabouts were the picture of health. He summoned his congregation to the town brewery where he plunged his ceremonial cross into the vat and told them: 'Don't drink the water, drink the beer.' The brewing process had of course killed off all the microbes in the water, added healthy proteins, vitamins and mineral salts, and everybody thrived – especially the brewers, who made Arnold their patron saint.

and snout, is another Flemish stew. *Lapin à la flamande* is rabbit marinated in beer and vinegar and braised in onions and prunes. High-quality game usually comes from the Ardennes including hare (*lièvre*), venison (*chevreuil*) and pheasant (*faisan*).

Vegetable dishes include *chou rouge à la flamande*, red cabbage cooked with apples, onions, red wine and vinegar; *chicon*, braised endives, often served *gratinée au four* (baked with cheese and ham); in the spring *asperges de Malines*, local white asparagus dressed with melted butter and crumbled hard-cooked egg; and *choux de Bruxelles* (brussels sprouts) often prepared with chestnuts, pieces of bacon and cooked in goose fat.

Among local **cheeses** are the very strong *remoudou*, the *djotte de Nivelles,* and cream cheeses from Brussels. Look out for the two-layered pancake with a tasty cheese filling, known as a *double*.

Strawberries and hot-house grapes usually appear on restaurant menus all year round.

If your sight-seeing gives you an appetite you will find a wide choice of snacks to tide you over.

Waffles (*gaufres*) are the best-known **dessert** of Belgian origin, but you should also try the *crêpes aux pommes* (apple pancakes), *beignets de Bruxelles* (a sort of doughnut or fritter), *tarte au riz* (rice tart), *manons* (chocolate filled with fresh cream), and the famous *speculoos* (spicy gingerbreads cut into shapes).

For those whose sweet tooth has not been satisfied yet, try the fine *pralines*, local chocolates of great subtlety in their **111**

De Gulden Boot

Y*ou'll be able to spend many happy hours sampling the different varieties of Belgian beer.*

flavour and variety. They are exported all over the world, but the best selection remains back in Brussels.

If you're looking for a small **snack** to tide you over until the next meal, then try the famous *frites*, available day and night at special stands (*friterie* or in Flemish *fritkot*) – and usually served in paper cones with salt and mayonnaise. *Caricoles* (sea snails) are another street speciality – eat them piping hot with the cup of spicy broth they were cooked in.

Drinks

With almost everything, you can drink St Arnold's favourite beverage, **Belgian beer**. There are four basic brews in the Brussels area, and all are made by a process of spontaneous fermentation, ie without yeast. The *Gueuze* is slightly sour in taste with a fine head of foam when poured; the *Lambic* is brewed in Bruegel's former stamping-grounds in the Senne valley south west of Brussels, a young beer without foam but plenty of strength; the *Faro* is a variety of *Lambic* with a much lower alcohol content; and finally, the bizarre *Kriek* is a reddish beer with the fruity taste of cherries added during the *Lambic's* fermentation.

You will also come across many sorts of *Trappiste*, a dark, strong malt beer brewed in Belgian monasteries, and *Pils*, a light beer brewed locally by fermentation at low temperatures.

Belgium itself produces a small number of **wines**, and the selections of French and German wines are often superior to what you might find in establishments in the countries of origin. The Belgians take pride in showing that they can appreciate good wine just as much as beer.

Belgian bars also serve strong alcoholic drinks such as whisky and liqueurs, and these are, of course, available in restaurants. Be sure to try the local gin, known as *pèket*.

To Help You Order...

	French	*Flemish*
Could we have a table?	**Pouvons-nous avoir une table?**	*Heeft u een tafel voor ons?*
Do you have a set menu?	**Avez-vous un menu du jour?**	*Heeft u een menu van de dag?*
I'd like a/an/some ...	**J'aimerais ...**	*Ik zou graag ... wille hebben.*
beer	**une bière**	*een pils*
butter	**du beurre**	*boter*
bread	**du pain**	*brood*
cheese	**du fromage**	*kaas*
coffee	**un café**	*koffie*
egg(s)	**un œuf(s)**	*een ei(eren)*
meat	**de la viande**	*vlees*
menu	**la carte**	*een menu*
milk	**du lait**	*melk*
mineral water	**de l'eau minérale**	*mineraal water*
salad	**une salade**	*sla*
sugar	**du sucre**	*de suiker*
tea	**du thé**	*thee*
wine	**du vin**	*wijn*

113

...and Read the Menu in French

agneau	lamb	**langue**	tongue
anguille	eel	**lapin**	rabbit
bœuf	beef	**lièvre**	hare
canard	duck	**moules**	mussels
champignons	mushrooms	**oie**	goose
chou	cabbage	**petit pois**	peas
choufleur	cauliflower	**pommes**	apples
choux de Bruxelles	Brussels sprouts	**pommes de terre**	potatoes
porc	pork	**poulet**	chicken
crevettes	shrimps	**pruneaux**	prunes
endives (chichon)	chicory (endive)	**raisins**	grapes
épinards	spinach	**ris de veau**	sweetbreads
faisan	pheasant	**riz**	rice
foie	liver	**rognons**	kidney
fraises	strawberries	**saucisse**	sausage
haricots verts	green beans	**truite**	trout
jambon	ham	**veau**	veal
		volaille	poultry

...and in Flemish

aardappelen	potatoes	**mosselen**	mussels
aardbeien	strawberries	**pruimen**	prunes
bloemkool	cauliflower	**rijst**	rice
druiven	grapes	**rodekool**	red cabbage
eend	duck	**rundvlees**	beef
forel	trout	**spruitjes**	Brussels sprouts
frieten (fries)	French fries		
garnalen	shrimps	**tong (vis)**	sole (fish)
haas	hare	**uien**	onions
kip	chicken	**varkensvlees**	pork
konijn	rabbit	**worst**	sausage

BLUEPRINT
for a
Perfect Trip

An A-Z Summary of Practical Information

> Listed after most main entries are the appropriate **French** and *Flemish* translations, usually in the singular. You'll find this vocabulary useful when asking for information or assistance.

A

ACCOMMODATION (See also CAMPING on p.118 and the list of RECOMMENDED HOTELS starting on p.65)

The hotels of Brussels cover the usual spectrum from luxurious and expensive to simple and cheap. In the absence of an official grading system, the capital's tourist office issues an annual hotel guide, listing approved hotels according to price and facilities. These hotels display a special shield. Room rates must be posted at the reception desk and in each room.

For hotel rooms in Brussels, you can reserve through the two tourist offices (see p.136). You can book hotel rooms in advance, anywhere in Belgium, through a free service offered by Belgian Tourist Reservations. Contact: BTR, 111 boulevard Anspachlaan, 1000 Brussels 23; tel. (02) 513 7484.

Apartments, bungalows and villas (furnished) can be rented for a holiday period, particularly in Brussels, the Ardennes and along the coast. Write to the local tourist office for full information.

Farmhouse arrangements are becoming increasingly popular – again, particularly in coastal regions and the Ardennes. Ask for the national tourist office's special brochure *Budget Holidays*.

Youth and student accommodation is available in both town and country. Some addresses are featured in the *Budget Holidays* brochure mentioned above, but for full details contact your national student travel organization or youth hostel association.

a double/single room	**une chambre à deux lits/à un lit**	*een tweepersoons-kamer/eenpersoons-kamer*
with/without bath	**avec/sans bains**	*met/zonder bad*
What's the rate per night?	**Quel est le tarif pour une nuit?**	*Hoeveel kost het per nacht?*

AIRPORT (aéroport/luchthaven)

Brussels National Airport at Zaventem, 12km (8 miles) north east of the capital, has the customary amenities, including duty-free shops (after passport control), a tourist information/hotel reservation service (in the arrivals area), and chapels and worship areas for all major faiths. Free baggage trolleys are plentiful, but porters scarce. Left-luggage (baggage-check) lockers are available in the arrivals area (near the post office).

Belgium proudly claims to have been the first country in the world to build a direct rail link between its national airport and the capital. Signs guide you down to the underground platform from which trains depart for Gare du Nord, Gare Centrale and Gare du Midi in Brussels from about 6am to midnight. There are three trains an hour for Gare du Nord and Gare Centrale, and one every hour for Gare du Midi. Purchase your ticket at the station or at the tourist information office in the baggage-claim hall. The trip takes 20 minutes.

An infrequent city bus service connects Zaventem with the Gare du Nord. Special Sabena buses connect Brussels Airport with Liège, Ghent, Antwerp and Hasselt/Maastricht. Taxis line up in front of the airport building. The trip to the centre of town will cost you quite a bit more than the train fare, but a 25% reduction in the taxi fare is available upon presentation of a round-trip air ticket.

For information about arriving and departing flights, call 723 2345 (for Sabena and cooperating airlines) or 723 0723 (for non-Sabena-affiliated airlines).

BICYCLE RENTAL

Steep hills, heavy traffic and inadequate cycle paths in the centre of Brussels will deter most would-be cyclists, but the Forêt de Soignes offers many bicycle paths through scenic woods. Cycle paths vary in availability and quality throughout the country. The best-equipped areas are Antwerp and West Flanders provinces. The *Yellow Pages* lists outlets under *Bicyclettes & cyclomoteurs/Fietsen & bromfietsen* (bicycles and mopeds). *Location* means rental.

Serviceable bikes can be rented at about 60 railway stations throughout the country. Rail travellers are given priority and reduced rates (show your train ticket). Phone ahead to the station to make your reservation – telephone numbers and further details are given in Belgian National Railways' brochure *Train + vélo/Trein + fiets*.

I'd like to hire a bicycle.	**J'aimerais louer une bicyclette.**	*Ik zou graag een fiets huren.*

CAMPING (See also MONEY MATTERS on p.131)

Belgium has more than 500 government-licensed campsites, graded in four categories. Most are located in the Ardennes and along the coast, but there are some sites in other parts of the country, a few within striking distance of the capital. Ask the Belgian National Tourist Office (see p.136) for its free camping brochure.

In some areas, particularly along the coast, camping is only permitted on recognized sites. Elsewhere, local farmers will often give you permission to pitch a tent or draw up a caravan (trailer) on their land for the night.

May we camp on your land, please?	**Pouvons-nous camper sur votre terrain, s'il vous plaît?**	*Mogen wij op uw terrain kamperen alstublieft?*

CAR RENTAL (*location de voitures/autoverhuring*)
(See also DRIVING IN BELGIUM on p.122 and MONEY MATTERS on p.131)

International and local rental firms are detailed in Brussels' *Yellow Pages*. The best-known companies have desks at the airport, but costs can be prohibitive. If time is available, you would be well advised to phone around for the best prices. Personnel usually speak English. Your home driving licence will be accepted provided you have held it for a year. The minimum age limit varies between 20 and 25, depending on the company and the vehicle you hire.

A credit card is by far the preferred means of payment. Collision insurance with the first BF30,000 deductible is available but expensive. Collision damage waivers and personal accident policies are available on request. There is no extra charge if you have the car delivered to your hotel in Brussels.

CLIMATE and CLOTHING

From the coast inland to Brussels, the Belgian climate is temperate maritime, similar to southeast England. The Ardennes has more continental weather, with warmer summers and colder winters. Rain can be expected at any time of year – and about every other day.

Average daytime temperatures in Brussels:

Temperature												
	J	F	M	A	M	J	J	A	S	O	N	D
°F	41	43	50	55	66	70	74	72	68	57	46	41
°C	5	6	10	13	19	21	23	22	20	14	8	6

Clothing. While business people in Brussels maintain a certain formality of dress, tourists need not be affected by this. Open-necked shirts and jeans are as popular here as anywhere. Only in the evenings, at better restaurants and hotels, are men required to wear a jacket (not necessarily a tie) and women usually dress up. Don't forget to take along a sweater or jacket for summer evenings. Warm clothing is essential in winter, and rainwear could be needed at any time of year. In clothes and shoe shops French, German, English and Belgian systems of measurement are all used, depending on the shop and article. Just ask the salesperson to size you up.

COMMUNICATIONS (see also OPENING HOURS on p.133)

Post offices. These are separate from Belgacom (telephone and tele-graph) offices. Look for the words *POSTES/POSTERIJEN* or *LA POSTE/DE POST* in shiny white letters on a red background. Open-ing hours vary (see OPENING HOURS on p.133). You may also pur-chase stamps at many news-stands, hotel lobbies, bookshops, street kiosks and vending machines. Mail boxes are red.

Poste restante (general delivery). If you're not sure where you'll be staying, have your mail sent to you *poste restante/poste-restante*, in care of the main post office in town (*poste principale/hoofdpostkan-toor*). For Brussels, the full address is: Mr John Smith, Poste Restante, Centre de la Monnaie, B-1000 Brussels. You'll have to show your passport and pay a nominal sum to retrieve mail.

Telegrams and faxes. During working hours, telegrams and faxes can be sent from Belgacom offices and most post offices, hotels, phone centres and railway stations. To send telegrams at night, at weekends or on public holidays, go to the Gare du Midi at 1 avenue Fonsny. You can also send telegrams by telephone by dialling 1325 or by fax by dialling 1335.

Have you any mail for ...?	**Avez-vous du courrier pour ...?**	*Hebt u post voor …?*
A stamp for this letter/postcard, please.	**Un timbre pour cette lettre/carte postale, s'il vous plaît.**	*Een postzegel voor deze brief/briefkaart, alstublieft.*
airmail	**par avion**	*luchtpost*
registered	**recommandé**	*aangetekend*
Can you get me this number in …?	**Pouvez-vous me donner ce numéro à ...?**	*Kunt u mij verbinden met dit nummer in …?*

Telephone. Away from your hotel, the Belgacom office is the place to make intercontinental calls or send telegrams. Larger towns have at least one Belgacom office. In Brussels, the offices are located at 17 Boulevard de l'Impératrice (near Gare Centrale) and at the airport.

Public telephone booths can be found at railway stations, post offices, in department stores and in the street. Those decorated with European national flags on the outside can be used for direct-dial international calls to most western European countries. Instructions are posted in English, Dutch, French and German. Go armed with a large stock of BF5 or BF20 coins. Many telephone booths take electronic cards called 'Telecard', easier to handle than coins. They can be purchased from post offices, news-stands and *librairies* (bookshops).

The *Yellow Pages* (*pages d'or/gouden gids*) covers all Belgian telephone districts. At the beginning of volume A you'll find indexes in English, Dutch, French and German. When dialling from outside the city, the area code for Brussels, including the airport, is 02.

COMPLAINTS

Brussels has many years' experience of catering for its visitors, and you are unlikely to encounter any major problems. If, however, you are not happy with a service or product, inform the relevant person on the spot. If you want to take a complaint further, go to the Tourist Office or, if appropriate, to the police.

CRIME (See also EMERGENCIES on p.125 and POLICE on p.134)

Standard precautions are in order in this generally unalarming city – deposit valuables and unneeded documents in your hotel safe, remove anything from your car that may tempt thieves, and lock it.

Pickpockets are a fact of life near the Grand-Place, the Bourse, in the Rue Neuve and at the Sunday market near Gare du Midi, where police loud-hail warnings to the throngs of shoppers. The sordid red-light district near Gare du Nord has its own risks after dark.

| I wish to report a theft. | **Je veux signaler un vol.** | *Ik wil aangifte doen van een diefstal.* |

CUSTOMS and ENTRY REGULATIONS

Most visitors, including nationals of Australia, Canada, New Zealand, Republic of Ireland, the UK and USA, need only a valid passport (no visa) to enter Belgium. British subjects can travel on the simplified Visitor's Passport.

Currency restrictions. There are no limitations on the import or export of either local or foreign currencies.

I've nothing to declare.	**Je n'ai rien à déclarer.**	*Ik heb niets aan te geven.*
It's for my personal use.	**C'est pour mon usage personnel.**	*Het is voor eigen gebruik.*

Duty-free allowance. The following shows the main duty-free items you may take into Belgium and back into your own country:

As Belgium is part of the EU (formerly EC), free exchange of non-duty free goods for personal use is permitted between Belgium and the UK and the Republic of Ireland. However, duty free items are still subject to restrictions: check before you go. For residents of non-EU countries, restrictions are as follows: Australia: 250 cigarettes or 250g tobacco; 1l alcohol; Canada: 200 cigarettes and 50 cigars and 400g tobacco; 1.1l spirits or wine or 8.5l beer; New Zealand: 200 cigarettes or 50 cigars or 250g tobacco; 4.5l wine or beer and 1.1l spirits; South Africa: 400 cigarettes and 50 cigars and 250g tobacco; 2l wine and 1l spirits; USA: 200 cigarettes and 100 cigars or a 'reasonable amount' of tobacco.

DRIVING IN BELGIUM
Entering Brussels. To bring your car into Belgium you will need:
- Your home driving licence (*permis de conduire/rijbewijs*) or an international driving licence.
- Car registration papers (*certificat d'immatriculation/uitschrijvingsbewijs*) and certificate of ownership, if available.

- Green Card or equivalent supplementary insurance making your policy valid for foreign countries.

You must have a national identity sticker visible on the back of the car, a fire extinguisher and a red warning triangle for use in case of breakdown. Drivers and all passengers are required by law to wear seat-belts. Children under 12 are not allowed in the front seat.

Speed limits. These are 120kph (74mph) on motorways, 90kph (55mph) on other roads and 50kph (31mph) in towns. Foreign visitors caught speeding can be made to pay on the spot.

Driving conditions. Drive on the right and pass on the left. At junctions, cars coming from the right have priority unless you are on a main road (marked with a sign displaying a yellow diamond or a broad arrow). Trams have priority at all times. When driving at night, headlights must be used in town. Your horn should only be used in case of emergency. Alcohol limit is 0.5g/l.

Superb, toll-free motorways, illuminated at night, criss-cross the country. These are designated as E roads (E411, E19, etc).

Traffic police, accidents. Patrol cars are white with a broad orange or blue stripe across the top from front to back, surmounted by a blue light. Increasingly, unmarked cars are also used. To contact the police, call 101 nationwide. Phone 105 for an ambulance.

Breakdowns. Three organizations handle breakdowns on the road:
Touring Club de Belgique, tel. (02) 233 2211
Royal Automobile Club de Belgique, tel. (02) 287 0900
Vlaamse Automobilistenbond (in Antwerp), tel. (03) 252 6270.

Emergency call boxes are usually sited at regular intervals along motorways. Black arrows on the poles of overhead lights indicate the direction of the nearest box.

Fuel and oil. Filling stations are plentiful, selling *super*, *normale/ normaal*, *sans plomb/loodvrij* (lead-free) and *gasoil/diesel*. Signs for '-30 cts', '-90 cts', etc. indicate that the station is selling petrol (gas) below the official recommended price by the amount indicated.

Parking. On the street, always park in the direction of moving traffic. Most Belgian cities have multi-storey car parks. Street parking arrangements vary. Signs marked 1-15 and 16-31 and bisected by a red slash mean that parking is not permitted on that side of the road on the dates noted. The Roman figures I and II indicate parking on alternate sides of the street on odd- and even-numbered days respectively. The blue zones require a special parking disk, available at garages, bookshops and news-stands. The sign 'CD' on the pavement or road indicates that street parking is reserved for diplomats.

Road signs. Most road signs are the standard pictographs used throughout Europe, but you could also encounter these written signs:

Soft shoulders	**Accotements non stabilisés**	*Zachte berm*
Caution	**Attention**	*Opgepast*
Other directions	**Autres directions**	*Andere richtingen*
Bad road surface	**Chaussée déformée/dégradée**	*Beschadigd wegdek*
Diversion (detour)	**Déviation**	*Wegomlegging*
Obstruction ahead	**Passage difficile**	*Moeilijke doorgang*
Toll	**Péage**	*Tol*
Slow	**Ralentir**	*Langzaam rijden*
One-way street	**Sens unique**	*Eenrichtingverkeer*
All directions	**Toutes directions**	*Alle richtingen*
Are we on the right road for…?	**Sommes-nous sur la route de …?**	*Zijn wij op de juiste wegnaar …?*
Fill the tank please.	**Le plein, s'il vous plaît.**	*Vol, graag.*
Check the oil/tyres/battery.	**Veuillez contrôler l'huile/les pneus/la batterie.**	*Kijkt u even de olie/banden/accu na.*
I've broken down.	**Ma voiture est en panne.**	*Ik heb autopech.*

Distance

Fluid measures

ELECTRIC CURRENT

All of Belgium is on 220-volt, 50-cycle AC.

EMBASSIES and CONSULATES (*ambassades; consulats/ambassades; consulaten*)

Diplomatic representations are grouped in the telephone directory under the above headings. Embassies in Brussels include:

Australia: 6 rue Guimard; tel. 231 0500

Canada: 2 avenue de Tervuren; tel. 741 0611

New Zealand: 47 boulevard du Régent; tel. 512 1040

Republic of Ireland: 19-21 rue Luxembourg; tel. 513 6633

South Africa: 26 rue de la Loi; tel. 230 6845

UK (consular department): 85 rue d'Arlon; tel. 287 6211

USA (consular section): 25 boulevard du Régent; tel. 513 3830

EMERGENCIES (*urgence/noodgeval*)
(See also POLICE on p.134)

The three-digit emergency telephone numbers listed on the following page are valid throughout the whole of Belgium. Other numbers are for Brussels only.

Emergency, police, gendarmerie **101**

Fire brigade and emergency ambulance **100**

Belgian Red Cross **105**

Ambulance 649 1122

Doctor (24 hours) 479 1818 or 648 8000

Pharmacy (evenings and weekends) 479 1818

Dentist (evenings and weekends) 426 1026

In Brussels, you can phone 648 4014 for general advice in English round the clock ('Help Line').

I need a doctor/ dentist.	**Il me faut un médecin/un dentiste**.	*Ik heb een arts/een tandarts nodig.*
hospital	**hôpital**	*ziekenhuis*

GAY and LESBIAN

There is a selection of gay and lesbian bars, cafés and discos in Brussels, as well as other establishments from saunas to cinemas. The TIB guidebook provides information on recommended venues, as do leaflets published by gay organizations. The English Gay Group is located at BP 198 – 1060 Brussels 6.

GUIDES and TOURS (*guide; interprète/gids; tolk*)
(See also MONEY MATTERS on p.131 and PLANNING YOUR BUDGET on p.132)

Most city sightseeing tours and excursions are accompanied by a multilingual guide. Before purchasing your ticket, make sure that English is offered. Tourist offices and private tour companies can supply guides for individuals and groups if you order in advance. Contact TIB at the Town Hall (tel. 513 8940) for information and reservations.

LANGUAGE

About 60% of Belgium (the northern half) speaks Flemish – or Dutch, which is the modern, written form of the language. French is the language in Wallonia, southern Belgium, and a small percentage of the people in eastern districts speak German.

In Brussels, an officially bilingual enclave in Dutch-speaking territory, about 80% of the native population speak French. Belgian French is virtually the same as that spoken in France, but the Walloons say *septante* and *nonante* instead of *soixante-dix* and *quatre-vingt-dix* (seventy and ninety).

Muster your school French or dabble in Dutch, and you'll find that taxi drivers, bar-hoppers and anyone else you come in contact with will appreciate your efforts and respond. Belgians will readily converse in whatever bits of languages they know.

You'll find that English is widely spoken in this European capital and it won't take you long to meet a resident English-speaker in cosmopolitan Brussels. Cafés, English-language churches and the capital's outdoor tavern terraces are the best places to meet people.

The Berlitz PHRASE BOOK AND DICTIONARY for French and Dutch cover most situations you're likely to encounter in your travels in Belgium. See also the Berlitz FRENCH–ENGLISH/ENGLISH–FRENCH POCKET DICTIONARY and the DUTCH–ENGLISH/ENGLISH–DUTCH POCKET DICTIONARY, each containing 12,500 terms plus a menu-reader supplement. You will also find a list of useful expressions on the front cover of this guide.

Place Names. Dozens of towns bear different names in French and Flemish, but in most parts of the country road signs are only in the language of the region you are in. Below is a list of some important equivalents (with the official name given first).

Aalst/Alost	**Liège**/Luik
Antwerpen/Anvers	**Mechelen**/Malines
Arlon/Aarlen	**Mons**/Bergen

Brugge/Bruges	**Namur**/Namen
De Haan/Le Coq	**Oostende**/Ostende
Dendermonde/Termonde	**Oudenaarde**/Audenarde
De Panne/La Panne	**Roeselare**/Roulers
Gent/Gand	**Ronse**/Renaix
Geraardsbergen/Grammont	**Tienen**/Tirlemont
Ieper/Ypres	**Tongeren**/Tongres
Koksijde/Coxyde	**Tournai**/Doornik
Kortrijk/Courtrai	**Wavre**/Waver
Leuven/Louvain	**Zoutleeuw**/Léau

SOME USEFUL EXPRESSIONS
(There are further useful expressions on the inside cover of this guide.)

	French	*Flemish*
Good evening	**Bonsoir**	*Goedenavond*
Goodbye	**Au revoir**	*Tot ziens*
where/when/how	**où/quand/comment**	*waar/wanneer/hoe*
today	**aujourd'hui**	*vandaag*
yesterday/tomorrow	**hier/demain**	*gisteren/morgen*
day/week	**jour/semaine**	*dag/week*
month/year	**mois/année**	*maand/jaar*
left/right	**gauche/droite**	*links/rechts*
good/bad	**bon/mauvais**	*goed/slecht*
cheap/expensive	**bon marché/cher**	*goedkoop/duur*
hot/cold	**chaud/froid**	*warm/koud*
open/closed	**ouvert/fermé**	*open/dicht*
entrance/exit	**entrée/sortie**	*entree/uitgang*
occupied/vacant	**occupé/libre**	*bezet/vrij*

Please write it down.	**Veuillez bien me l'écrire.**	*Wilt u het alstublieft opschrijven?*
What does this mean?	**Que signifie ceci?**	*Wat betekent dit?*

LAUNDRY and DRY-CLEANING (*blanchisserie; nettoyage à sec* or *teinturier/wasserij; stomerij*)

Establishments can be found in all parts of town, some of which (like the larger hotels) offer same-day service. They are all listed in the Brussels *Yellow Pages*. For a more economical wash, try a laundromat (*salon-lavoir/wasserette* or *wassalon*).

When will it be ready?	**Quand est-ce que ce sera prêt?**	*Wanneer is het klaar?*
I must have it for tomorrow morning.	**Il me le faut pour demain matin.**	*Ik heb dit morgenvroeg nodig.*

LOST PROPERTY

Your first line of inquiry, anywhere in Belgium, would generally be the police. In Brussels, phone the *service des objets trouvés/gevonden voorwerpen* on 517 9675. Other lost property offices:

Airport: tel. 723 6011 (objects lost on the aeroplane), tel. 722 3940 (objects lost in the airport).

Railway: tel. 219 2640 if the number and destination of the train are known, otherwise 224 6112 one week later, from 7.30 am to 7.15pm.

Public transport: located in the Porte de Namur métro station, tel. 515 2394, from 9.30am to 12.30pm.

Taxi drivers usually hand things in to the police or their head office.

I've lost my …	**J'ai perdu mon …**	*Ik ben mijn … kwijt*
wallet	**portefeuille**	*portefeuille*
handbag	**sac à main**	*handtas*
passport	**passeport**	*paspoort*

MEDIA

Television. Belgian cable TV feeds as many as 30 stations into most sets. Domestic telecasts are in both French and Dutch, and the bonus programmes come from Britain (BBC1, BBC2, MTV, Superchannel), France, Germany, Luxembourg, Italy, Spain, USA and the Netherlands. Euronews is broadcast regularly on TV5.

Radio. English-language broadcasts include the US Armed Forces Network on 101.7 FM and the BBC World Service on 648 medium wave/AM.

Newspapers and magazines (*journal*; *revue/krant*; *tijdschrift*). Leading foreign newspapers and magazines are available at shops and news-stands in the centre of Brussels and other large cities. The British press is particularly well represented, and Americans will be able to keep up to date with the Paris-based *International Herald Tribune* and Brussels-edited *Wall Street Journal/Europe*.

For an English-language round-up of local activities, events and news, buy *The Bulletin*, a weekly magazine with regular features.

| Have you any English-language newspapers? | **Avez-vous des journaux en anglais?** | *Heeft u Engelse kranten?* |

MEDICAL CARE (See also EMERGENCIES on p.125)

Medical care is of the highest standard but expensive, so it's worth making sure that your normal health insurance covers foreign journeys. British nationals enjoy reduced-rate treatment in case of injury or accident in Belgium. Many doctors speak English.

Pharmacies (*pharmacie/apotheek*) are easily recognized by a green cross. A few pharmacies stay open in each neighbourhood after hours and at week-ends. The list is posted outside each one and published in the weekend editions of the local newspapers.

Where's the duty pharmacy?	**Où est la pharmacie de garde?**	*Waar is de dienstdoende apotheek?*

MONEY MATTERS

Currency. The unit of Belgian currency is the *franc* (in French) and *de frank* (in Dutch), abbreviated BF or FB (BF in this guide). It is divided into 100 centimes (cts). **Coins** in circulation: 50cts, BF1, BF5, BF20 and BF50; **banknotes**: BF100, BF500, BF1,000, BF2,000 and BF10,000. (**Note**. The BF2,000 has replaced the BF5,000, which can now be exchanged only at the Banque Nationale de Belgique.)

The Luxembourg franc, at parity with Belgian currency, circulates freely in Belgium and, though always accepted, is not very popular. Watch out for it in your change.

Banks (*banque/bank*) **and currency exchange** (*bureau de change/wisselkantoor*). Branches are plentiful in city centres, seaside resorts, at railway stations and at the airport; these give a better rate than hotels, shops and restaurants. In the Brussels area, some currency-exchange facilities are open on Sundays and public holidays. See OPENING HOURS section. Currency-exchange machines at the airport make transactions in four currencies.

Traveller's cheques (*chèque de voyage/reischeque*) are widely accepted throughout Belgium. When you change traveller's cheques, a standard, flat-rate minimum charge is made every time, so don't cash them in dribs and drabs. Take your passport along when you go to change money. There is a machine which cashes American Express cards and traveller's cheques at the airport.

Eurocheques are accepted by a wide range of businesses, including motorway filling stations.

Credit cards (*carte de crédit/credit card*) are accepted in many hotels, restaurants, shops, etc. Signs indicate which cards are accepted.

Sales tax, service charge. Called TVA/BTW, a sales (value-added) tax is imposed on all goods and services. In hotels and restaurants, **131**

this is accompanied by a service charge. The sign 'Service et TVA in-clus/Service en BTW inbegrepen' tells you that services and TVA/BTW are included in the price. Enquire if you are eligible for a TVA refund on more expensive purchases.

I want to change some pounds/dollars.	**Je voudrais changer des livres sterling/ dollars.**	*Ik wil graag ponden/dollars wisselen.*
Do you accept travel-ler's cheques?	**Acceptez-vous les chèques de voyage?**	*Accepteert u reis-cheques?*
Can I pay with this credit card?	**Puis-je payer avec cette carte de crédit?**	*Kan ik met deze credit card betalen?*

PLANNING YOUR BUDGET

To give you an idea of what to expect, here's a list of average prices in Belgian francs (BF). They can only be approximate, however, as inflation continues to push prices up.

Airport transfer. Train (second class) to city centre BF85, taxi BF800 from Central Station.

Baby-sitters. BF200 per hour.

Buses, trams and métro. Single ticket BF50, card of 5 tickets BF230, card of 10 tickets BF305, 24-hour card BF120.

Camping. BF250-400 for a family of four for one night.

Car hire. *Opel Corsa LS* BF1,500 per day; BF15 per km; BF13,000 per week. *Ford Sierra GL* BF2,300 per day; BF23 per km; BF18,500 per week. *Audi 100* (*auto*) BF2,550 per day; BF26 per km; BF31,000 per week. All weekly rentals with unlimited mileage. Add 25% tax.

Cigarettes. BF105 for a packet of 20.

Entertainment. Cinema BF220 (cheaper on Mondays), ballet/opera BF700-2,200, discotheque/nightclub BF250 and above.

Guides. BF2,600 per half day (3 hours); BF4,800 (plus lunch) per day.

Hairdressers. *Man's* cut, shampoo and styling BF600. *Woman's* cut and blow-dry BF1,400; shampoo and set BF800.

Hotels (double room with bath and breakfast, per night). Luxury BF6,000-7,000; moderate BF2,600-3,500; budget BF2,000. Youth hostels BF400 plus sheet rental per night with breakfast.

Meals and drinks. Breakfast BF250, lunch BF350, 'typical' dinner (steak, French fries, salad) BF600, bottle of wine BF300-400, beer from BF40, soft drink BF50, coffee BF50.

Shopping. Hand-made lace handkerchief BF400-800, Belgian chocolates per kilo BF400-800.

Taxis. Meter charge BF95 (BF170 at night), plus BF38 per km inside the city (BF76 per km outside), plus waiting time BF600 per hour.

Tours. Group tour of Brussels centre (half day) BF700, boat tour of port of Antwerp BF300.

Trains. Ostend-Brussels (second class, one way) BF425, Brussels-Antwerp BF180, Brussels-Bruges BF355.

OPENING HOURS (see also PUBLIC HOLIDAYS on p.135)
All hours given here must be regarded as approximate, as schedules – even for public services such as the post office – vary considerably.

Banks. Generally open from 9am to 3.30 or 4pm Monday to Friday. A few are open Saturday morning. Some banks are open until 6pm two days a week. Small branches may close for lunch.

Currency-exchange offices. Those at Brussels airport open from 7am to 9.45pm and those at Gare du Midi and Gare du Nord operate from 7am to 10.45pm every day of the year. The office at Gare Centrale is open from 8am to 9pm every day.

Museums. Usually open from 10am to 5pm Tuesday to Sunday, sometimes with a one-hour lunchtime closure somewhere between noon and 2pm. Closed on Mondays and some public holidays.

Offices and businesses. From 9am to 5pm Monday to Thursday; 9am to noon Friday.

Post offices. Hours are normally from 9am to 5pm Monday to Friday. The post office at Gare du Midi (48a avenue Fonsny) is open 24 hours a day, every day of the year, while the office at the airport is open from 7.15am to 9.45pm daily. Smaller offices, particularly in some rural areas, may take a lunchtime break and also close earlier in the afternoon.

Shops. Department stores generally open from 9am to 7pm, six days a week, closing late one evening (Friday in Brussels). Smaller shops may close over lunch and stay open later.

Telephone/telegraph offices. The office at the Gare du Midi at 1 avenue Fonsny is open 24 hours every day. The Belgacom office at 17 boulevard de l'Impératrice is open every day from 8am to 10pm.

P

PHOTOGRAPHY

All types of film are widely available, and developing and printing are of high quality. Colour processing can be done in one hour. Enlargements take a day. Airport security machines use X-rays, which can ruin your film on repeated exposure if it is not in a film-shield. Using a flash is forbidden in many museums and, in some, cameras are banned altogether. Many monuments are illuminated at night.

I'd like a film for this camera.	**J'aimerais un film pour cet appareil.**	*Mag ik een film voor dittoestel?*
How long will it take to develop this film?	**Combien de temps faut-il pour développer ce film?**	*Hoe lang duur het ontwikkelen van deze film?*

POLICE (See also EMERGENCIES on p.125)

Police officers come in two varieties: the municipal *police/politie* and the *gendarmerie/rijkswacht*. As a rule, the *police* are responsible for law and order, while the *gendarmerie* deal with large-scale operations such as crowd control, traffic supervision and motorway patrol. Dial 101 for information or assistance.

Where's the nearest police station?	**Ou est le commissariat de police le plus proche?**	*Waar is het dichtsbijzijnde politiebureau?*

PUBLIC HOLIDAYS (*jour férié/openbare feestdag*)

If a holiday falls on a Sunday, the following Monday is taken off instead. These public holidays are observed throughout the country:

January 1	New Year's Day	*Jour de l'An/Nieuwjaar*
May 1	Labour Day	*Fête du Travail/Dag van de arbeid*
July 21	National Day	*Fête Nationale/Nationale-feestdag*
August 15	Assumption	*Assomption/Maria Hemelvaart*
November 1	All Saints' Day	*Toussaint/Allerheiligen*
November 11	Armistice Day	*Anniversaire de l'Armistice/ Wapenstilstand*
December 25	Christmas Day	*Noel/Kerstdag*
Movable dates:	Easter Monday	*Lundi de Pâques/Paasmaandag*
	Ascension	*Ascension/Hemelvaartsdag*
	Whit Monday	*Lundi de Pentecote/ Pinkstermaandag*

R

RELIGION (*office religieux/kerkdienst*)

Though Belgium is a predominantly Roman Catholic country, Protestant denominations are quite well represented. You can attend English-language services at many churches in Brussels. There are **135** mosques and synagogues, but services are not in English. Inquire at your hotel reception desk, or phone 511 2715 or 511 8178 between 10am and 6pm, Monday to Saturday.

TIME DIFFERENCES

The following chart shows the time difference between Belgium and various cities in winter. Between April and September Belgian clocks are put forward one hour:

New York	London	Belgium	Jo'burg	Sydney	Auckland
6am	11am	noon	1pm	10pm	midnight

TIPPING

Service charge is included in hotel and restaurant bills and in taxi fares, but you should tip bellboys, maids, etc. for their services. Some suggestions:

Barber	20%
Cinema usher	BF20 per person
Hairdresser	20% (if service charge not included)
Lavatory attendant	BF10-15
Maid, per week	BF100-150
Hotel porter, per bag	BF30
Tour guide	10%

TOURIST INFORMATION OFFICES

Branches of the Belgian National Tourist Office will be of great help in planning your trip.

UK: 5th Floor, 29 Prince Street, London, W1R 7RG;
tel. (0891) 887 799.

USA: 745 Fifth Avenue, New York, NY 10022;
tel. (212) 758 8130.

The headquarters of the Belgian National Tourist Office are located at 63 rue Marché-aux-Herbes, 1000 Brussels; tel. (02) 504 0390.

The Tourist and Information Office of Brussels (TIB) is situated in the Town Hall (Hôtel de Ville) at Grand-Place, 1000 Brussels; tel. (02) 513 8940. There is also an information centre in the airport, by the baggage-claim area.

| Where is the tourist office? | **Où est l'office du tourisme?** | *Waar is het verkeers-bureau?* |

In virtually all Belgian towns you'll find a tourist office near the railway station or central square. Signs to look for:

Office du tourisme	*Verkeersbureau*
Syndicat d'initiative	*Informatiebureau*
Renseignements	*Inlichtingen*

TRANSPORT (See also MONEY MATTERS on p.131)

The Brussels public transport system is an integrated network of underground (subway), tram (streetcar) and bus routes providing excellent coverage of the capital and immediate surroundings. Free route maps are available at the tourist offices, at STIB (Société des Transports Intercommunaux de Bruxelles) underground information centres at Porte de Namur, Rogier and Gare du Midi, at any metro station and at the STIB offices at 15 avenue Toison d'Or. For information phone 515 2000.

The **underground** (*métro/metro*) consists of two lines: one crossing from east to west and the other (the *petite ceinture),* winding its way in several different directions. Stations are indicated by a large blue M sign, and decorated inside with paintings, sculpture and ceramics.

Trams serve most of the city and link up usefully with the métro; lines which can be used by both are called *pré-métro/premetro*.

Buses are of two kinds. Yellow and blue ones operate only within the city limits, orange/yellow or white ones go out to the suburbs. All-night buses (*bus de nuit/nachtbus*) provide a skeleton service on a **137**

limited number of routes. All stops are 'on request' only (*Arrêt sur demande/Halte op verzoek*) – to board the vehicle, make a sign with the hand; to get off, push the button.

Individual tickets and five-ride tickets, allowing you up to an hour's travel on any combination of tram, bus and métro within the city limits, can be purchased on buses and trams and in métro stations. Keep your ticket until you complete your journey.

With a 'Go as you please' ticket you have the run of the public transport system (bus, métro, tram – but not trains) for a whole day in any of 25 Belgian cities and towns. You can buy them at métro stations, STIB information offices, tourist offices and newsagents.

Taxis wait at ranks outside stations, large hotels and other key points throughout the city. You can also order taxis by telephone. Taxis are metered and the price shown is all-inclusive for any number of passengers. The per-kilometre rate doubles for a Brussels-based cab once it leaves the city limits, and there is an additional charge of BF75 at night. Inquire, about flat-rate charges to the airport. There is no extra charge for luggage.

Trains (*train/trein*) are classed as I/C (Intercity), I/R (Inter-regional), P (Rush-hour service) and L (Local) in descending order of rapidity. Tourist trains (T) provide express service during peak periods. The capital's five main railway stations are Gare du Nord and Gare Centrale for domestic and international trains and the shuttle service to the airport, Gare du Midi for domestic and international trains, Gare de Schaerbeek for car-carrying trains and Gare du Quartier Léopold for domestic trains and all departures for Luxembourg.

The *B-Tourrail* entitles the holder to five days' unrestricted travel for a period of one month anywhere in Belgium. The Benelux-Tourrail ticket gives the same privileges in the three countries (Belgium, the Netherlands and Luxembourg). See also BY RAIL on p.139.

When's the next bus/ train to ...?	**Quand part le prochain bus/train pour ...?**	*Wanneer vertrekt de volgende bus/trein naar ...?*

I want a ticket to ...	**J'aimerais un billet pour ...**	*Ik wil graag een kaartjenaar ...*
single (one way)	**aller simple**	*enkele reis*
return (round-trip)	**aller et retour**	*retour*
first/second class	**première/deuxième classe**	*eerste/tweede klas*

TRAVELLING TO BELGIUM

The choice of routes and fares to Belgium is so varied that the services of a knowledgeable travel agent are indispensable.

By Air. Brussels airport (see AIRPORT p.117) is linked by direct flights from most European and many North American cities. Travellers from further afield may have to connect via Paris, Amsterdam or London. Enquire about reductions on scheduled flights.

A fly-and-drive arrangement (with rental car at the airport) is particularly useful if you also plan to see the environs of Brussels.

By Sea and Road. The jet foil (foot-passengers only) goes from Ramsgate to Ostend in 95 minutes. Longer, but with car-carrying facilities, are the ferry crossings from Ramsgate to Ostend. Hovercraft services run from Folkstone to Boulogne and from Dover to Calais. There are also car and passenger ferries from Ramsgate to Dunkirk and from Hull to Zeebrugge.

By Coach. There are direct coach services to Brussels from major European cities and from London and several provincial centres in Britain.

By Rail. The *Eurostar* train runs frequently between London and Brussels taking under 4½ hours. Visitors living outside Europe and North Africa can purchase a *Eurailpass* for unlimited first-class rail travel in 16 European countries, including Belgium (not UK). Anyone under 26 years of age can get the second-class *Eurail Youthpass*. These tickets must be bought before leaving home. Those under 26 are also entitled to purchase an *Inter-Rail* card which allows 15 days or one month's unlimited second-class travel in Europe.

139

The *Rail Europ S* (senior) card, obtainable in Belgium before departure only, entitles senior citizens to purchase train tickets for European destinations at reduced prices.

Any family of at least three people can buy a *Rail-Europ F* (family) card: the holder pays full price, the rest of the family obtain a 50% reduction in Belgium and 14 other European countries; the whole family is also entitled to a 30% reduction on Sealink and Hoverspeed Channel crossings.

TRAVELLERS WITH DISABILITIES

The Tourist and Information Office of Brussels (TIB) publications indicate which tourist venues, hotels and restaurants provide wheelchair access. (See p.45 for details on disabled access to museums.)

WEIGHTS AND MEASURES

(For fluid and distance measures, see DRIVING on p.125). Belgium uses the metric system.

Length

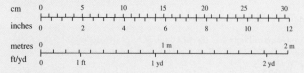

Temperature

Weight

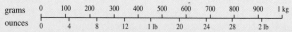

Index

Where there is more than one set of references, the one in **bold** refers to the main entry. References in *italics* refer to an illustration.

144